INTER
VIEWS

By the same author

EMOTION

SUICIDE AND THE SOUL

THE MYTH OF ANALYSIS

RE-VISIONING PSYCHOLOGY

LOOSE ENDS

INSEARCH: PSYCHOLOGY
AND RELIGION

THE DREAM AND THE
UNDERWORLD

AN ESSAY ON PAN

HEALING FICTION

ARCHETYPAL PSYCHOLOGY:
A BRIEF ACCOUNT

INTER VIEWS

**CONVERSATIONS WITH LAURA POZZO
ON PSYCHOTHERAPY, BIOGRAPHY, LOVE,
SOUL, DREAMS, WORK, IMAGINATION,
AND THE STATE OF THE CULTURE**

by JAMES HILLMAN
with LAURA POZZO

HARPER COLOPHON BOOKS
Harper & Row, Publishers
New York, Cambridge, Philadelphia, San Francisco
London, Mexico City, São Paulo, Sydney

"Laura Pozzo" is a pseudonym.

A hardcover edition of this book is published by Harper & Row, Publishers, Inc.

INTER VIEWS. Copyright © 1983 by James Hillman. All rights reserved. Printed in the United States of America. No part of this book may be used or reproduced in any manner whatsoever without written permission except in the case of brief quotations embodied in critical articles and reviews. For information address Harper & Row, Publishers, Inc., 10 East 53rd Street, New York, N.Y. 10022. Published simultaneously in Canada by Fitzhenry & Whiteside Limited, Toronto.

First HARPER COLOPHON edition published 1984.

Designed by Ruth Bornschlegel

Library of Congress Cataloging in Publication Data

Hillman, James.
  Inter views.
  Includes index.
  1. Psychoanalysis. 2. Psychology. I. Pozzo, Laura II. Title.
BF175.H46 1983   150   82-48119
ISBN 0-06-091128-X (pbk.)

84 85 86 87 88 10 9 8 7 6 5 4 3 2 1

CONTENTS

AUTHORS' PREFACE

In the summer of 1980 I took the plane from Rome to Zurich to keep an appointment with James Hillman that we had made by correspondence. The publishing house of Laterza in Bari, Italy, had agreed to my proposal of interviewing James Hillman on depth psychology, psychotherapy, and the state of the culture for their series of small books by leading intellectuals discussing in this format their views of present conditions. I had already worked on the R. D. Laing volume and became interested in the work of James Hillman. Translations of his work had been published in Italian, archetypal psychology was getting officially known and recorded in the *Italian Encyclopedia of the Twentieth Century,* and *The Myth of Analysis* and *Pan and the Nightmare* were bestsellers. As an acknowledgment of his renown, in 1981 Hillman was awarded the Medal of the Commune of Florence for the links he established between new directions in psychological thinking and the psychology of the Florentine Renaissance.

The Italian concerns in the ensuing interview, however, are not directed only at an Italian audience. They express the fundamental orientation of Hillman's work toward a psychology which he calls "Mediterranean" or "Southern" in its cultural sources, its themes, and its vistas—that is, mythical, passionately intellectual, aesthetic, and urban. The idea of Italy as a wide-ranging imaginal territory for this kind of psychology was intriguing. To me, Hillman's attempt was a new instance of the Italian journey of the Northern imagination. This psychology that Hillman refers to as "a therapy of imagination which re-imagines therapy" had, to my mind, great relevance for Italy, and beyond.

My background is mostly in literature, both Renaissance and modern—my field of study and research at the University of Rome—and in psychology—Freudian and Jungian. I also write, translate, and review, and it was as an independent journalist that I had the idea of the interview. I brought along to Switzerland specific questions and broad themes, and I was curious to see what would come out of the venture: I really did not foresee what I was getting into.

Hillman—who had moved back to America (Dallas, Texas, in 1978) after thirty years in Europe—was again in Europe en route to the Eranos Conference in Ascona. He had set aside parts of five days for taping. We met in a quiet flat and paused only for meals. Not only the machine but our conversation broke down again and again—our struggle was with the paradigm itself: the interview as a form, the question-answer interlocution as inappropriate for a psychology of soul, the notion of biography, and the interference of a lively imagination in a rational discussion.

Later, when I typed out the tapes and began their translation into Italian, it became evident that we would have to meet again. There were too many spots and holes and too many repetitions. These subsequent meetings took place in Rome in February and in Ascona in October, 1981. What emerges here is due not only to our enjoyable cooperation but especially to the care James gave afterward to the editing of the texts.

LAURA POZZO

From the beginning the idea for this book was Laura Pozzo's, and the topics, as formed into these chapters, also hers. She arrived at our first meeting with a definite plan to which we mainly adhered. Her broad cultural background, her many languages, and her specific knowledge of my writings allowed me freedom to leap beyond explaining the basics: I didn't have to begin in, repeat, square one. As an interviewer, she kept to the spartan single voice, thereby graciously inviting multiple and luxuriant responses to come through from my side. The final version has been helped by Patricia Berry and Hope Harris. Laura and I both thank our editors, Hugh Van Dusen and Janet Goldstein.

JAMES HILLMAN

INTER VIEWS

1 ON THE INTERVIEW

L.P. *You seem to be very uneasy about doing this interview. Why?*

J.H. I have a strange feeling about the whole business. I am distrustful about journalism, interviews. I have never been able to do it on television or radio, an interview was always some kind of clutchy thing. Also I have a tremendously strong feeling that the work is ten times more interesting than the person, and interviews are not particularly helpful in regard to the work: they may even steal from it, cheat it, waste it. I believe *in the work*.

L.P. *I don't intend to separate you from your work. That's why we are here. The archetypal psychology which you have developed out of Jung has some of the most important cultural ideas in our day. It's a revolution in psychology in every sort of way—the style of thinking and writing, the classic tradition it comes from in myth, in literature, in Platonic philosophy, the way you view psychopathology, the sense of what you call "soul" all through your works. . . . I want us to explore the work.*

J.H. But the work is available—the books are there. And the work takes so much work to get the way you want it. You can never get it that way in a conversation; it's too easy—unless the conversation hits a certain peak. . . .

L.P. *Why did you accept this interview, then?*

J.H. Last year I tried again to get out of the *Schreibstube,* that closet of introversion, sitting and writing and practicing. I went around America, talking and listening to questions. The questions forced me to think things, say things. Things came right out of my throat, and I was fascinated listening to what was coming up, like the throat could say new things and different things than what comes from my hands when I'm writing. Then, there's another reason: I am very interested in what goes on in Italy.

L.P. *Why so?*

J.H. Because I like to think my work is written out of a Mediterranean fantasy.

L.P. *What do you mean by "a Mediterranean fantasy"?*

J.H. This has to do partly with, let's say, the Renaissance, that I'm now trying to bring back a style of thought which has to do with "figure"—persons, figures, rhetoric, style—with a psychology that's not conceptual. All these things enter somehow in my fantasy of Italy. But this is my *fantasy* of Italy.

L.P. *Can you explain this more clearly? It is quite difficult for an Italian to accept being a fantasy though Italians have always and everywhere been fantasized about.*

J.H. Well, it is not that I am "making up" the Italians; it simply is that there is a geography that's physical and there's a geography that's imaginational. Shakespeare had an imagination of Italy, so he put all kinds of things in Italy, and Nietzsche had an imagination of Italy, Goethe had an imagination of Italy, Jung had big dreams located in Italy. Italy has suffered from the Northern imagination or profited from the Northern imagination for centuries. So I have an "Italian" imagination, a fantasy that the Italian mind, heart, or *anima* responds to a more aesthetic kind of thinking. For me to write from a Mediterranean fantasy means to let aesthetic considerations play a big part; I don't care so much if I make mistakes like being sentimental or cloudy or decorative or overcomplicated and baroque or trapped by traditional forms and words—let's call these "Italian" mistakes. They are anyway better than German, Northern mistakes, or that French foolishness about clarity and their semantic obsessions. I always loved your Vico for his hatred of Descartes and the French mind. America has the "French disease"—structuralism, Lacanism, Derrida, and when they don't have that they get German measles: Heidegger, Hesse, to say nothing of Germanic depth psychology.... I wish they once could get infected by Italy.

L.P. *I wonder whether your "Italy" and those Italian "mistakes" belong to the Italy I know or to a literary fantasy you need in* *order to do what you want to do. I suppose you have to have a "place," a geographical soil to grow your thoughts from.*

J.H.   That's good. Yes. But there is something else about Italy that I ought to confess. For me it's truly the society in that state of *Umbruch,* as the Germans would call it, breaking apart, falling apart; and that falling apart is utterly real, right in the streets. At the same time much more mental life seems to be going on in Italy than, say, in Germany. You print more new book titles, more translations than Germany or England or France. Partly because of this falling apart, this breakdown, ideas become necessities, not luxuries. How you think and what you think in Italy is extremely important because it determines how you are. So a psychological idea becomes not only a mode of self-discovery in a subjectivist way, like the "me" culture in California. In Italy psychological ideas go beyond the "me" culture to the whole culture, to how to live, because you are up against the problem of living. Experience, you could say—but I don't use that word, it's too abstract—it's being shot in the street or kidnapped or friends being taken by the police or God knows what, something is happening so that your intellect is immediately engaged. Like in the Renaissance. You can't help but be engaged. And that is part of what I call aesthetic—immediate sense-awareness, like an animal who lives by sense-intelligence. And also in Italy there is an entire collective consciousness that's going through something. And it is probably going through two thousand years of the Church in a very short span of time, confronting the old Christian culture with the new: for me the whole Western culture is there like in a microcosm, in Italy more than anywhere else. . . . Goodness, I'm already in the interview and don't want to be.

See, this is just what I don't like. It's *inflating.* I'm telling you all about Italy—and what do I know about Italy! It's *your* country.

L.P.   *It's your Italian fantasy, your fantasy-Italy. But why is an interview inflating?*

J.H.   Because I am being asked direct ego questions, and I answer out of the top of my head, and I spout off opinions. When you write, you can work them through. Like this, they come out too self-importantly. I'm afraid the whole endeavor will just inflate us both. You know that talk just by itself is inflating—sitting around for hours in a cafe, the old Mediterranean habit, can keep your spirit up. It's like a drug.

L.P. *So it's not only that you don't like the interview, it's that you are afraid of going up, getting high on it.*

J.H. That's because an interview has a certain style and that style is counterindicated for psychology as I see it. Interviews belong to an ego genre: one ego asking another ego. So one thinks one has to proceed in terms of "I answer a question" and "stick to the topic," "the given subject," and one tries to say it *knapp,* you know, nicely, tightly, rationally. "Directed thinking" it's called in psychiatry. All ego. Now, the kind of psychology that I want to do is not addressed to the ego. It is to evoke imagination, it's to be extremely complex, it's to talk with emotion and from emotion and to emotion; so how can you, in an interview, bring in that complexity? How can you speak to the whole psyche at the same time? When I write something, I'm conscious that I touch a theme in the second page or third page and I'm not going to take that up again for a long time, and I pick it up later on; the whole work of writing a paper or an article or a chapter is always consciously elaborated, consciously formed, in terms of an art work. . . . Now, what's the art work of an interview? I don't know what it is! . . . The rhetoric of an interview is an ego-rhetoric, and I'm paralyzed in that style. I can't use my whole palette, I have to cut everything out and answer the one question. It becomes monotheistic thinking and I can't do it. I can't do monotheistic thinking. One of my friends says there are three things for a psychologist to avoid: the panel discussion, the talk show, and the interview. No depth.

L.P. *Interesting to watch you attack and destroy the very area we are working in. Your remarks now against the interview are part of your method. When you write on any subject at all, and I am thinking of your paper on parapsychology or your book on suicide or even on Jung and Freud, you always first clear the area with an attack on the subject itself, as if it isn't worth doing or it is impossible to do. You build your structure by destructuring not* merely the ideas in a field but the field itself—in this case the interview.

J.H. Don't you have to start off by seeing the hopelessness first? If we begin with a hidden assumption that we know what we are doing, if we begin with enthusiasm, we'll fall on our faces.

L.P. *We could let the hopelessness in as irony. . . .*

J.H. I like that: the irony of this interview is that it is hopeless. That's a nice start—right in the pathology.

L.P. *I was thinking more of Platonic irony, that we are like characters in a dialogue being imagined by an author, and the author would be knowing where we are going while the characters would not. They would be feeling hopeless even though they were actually carrying the action forward.*

J.H. It's the part that doesn't know that interests me, because that means just letting the characters speak, the throat. But an interview isn't a classical dialogue. There's no author. Everyone knows a classical dialogue is a piece of fiction, but our conversation is supposed to be spontaneous, cinema verité, just like it is. Literally real—and, damn it, I don't want to enter anything that is literally real. It's like being in court, where you answer questions, bringing material evidence for your point of view, defending your position. So, the best we can do is pretend it is literally real, pretend we are now doing that kind of piece called "an interview."

L.P. *This seems like sophistry, even cheating. What about the reader who bought the book? Is it decent to pretend that we are doing something that we are not? He expects some truth, and he has the right to expect it.*

J.H. The reader is very much in mind. We couldn't be doing this without him—or her. Maybe we have to speak directly to this reader, right now: Reader, please don't stop listening, please don't get angry, please don't think we are putting you on. Let me explain: I am really a writer and it is hard to speak directly. I don't really have the courage to speak right out. I have to do it in my closet, by writing. When I am asked a question directly, in con-

frontation, I am a coward. So the interview isn't my style. I usually write letters to my friends and to my children rather than say
things straight out. I need some kind of ruse between me and
you in order to be sincere. I need sophistication just so not to be a
sophist.

L.P. *There is a beautiful sentence by Kafka that says something
like "Confession and lie are the same thing. We cannot commu-
nicate what we are, exactly because we are it. We can communi-
cate only what we are not: that is, only the lie." We cannot com-
municate what we are exactly because truth and sincerity are not
the same thing. So you can tell the truth without being sincere.*

J.H. Truth is revealed. It cannot ever be told. We cannot tell the
truth. It has to appear inside the telling or through the telling.
That's why we listen to what's *not* said in psychoanalysis, and
that's again what goes wrong in an interview: It focuses too much
on what's said.

L.P. *But the reader doesn't have to focus on what's said. He can
read the interview like a psychoanalyst—or like Kafka or Oscar
Wilde, who also wrote on the value of lying.*

J.H. Sometimes we think naively that when we are sincere, or
"straight," as we call it in America, then that is the truth. But the
whole truth and nothing but the truth, as we say too in America,
includes lots of other rhetorical styles like sophistication, irony,
fictions, even half-truths. It reminds me of that short story by
Thomas Mann where the young German officer reads his poetry
aloud and it's a disaster because it's so sincere; no artfulness.
Once I was entertained on a lecture tour and the host asked me
over a very quiet refined dinner, like the salon where the officer
read his poems, who I really was and that he wanted to meet the
real me. Well, I got enraged, right there at the table, and slammed
my hand down. It was awful because it had been such a nice
quiet dinner. You see, it implied that all I wrote, all I did when I
stood up and lectured—naked and sweating and putting myself
out and anxious, the whole thing—wasn't the "real me." Thomas
Mann knew what he was doing in that story, in all his stories
about art—you just are no one when you are sincerely really
"you." Truth has to have veils. It needs the protection of irony.

This interview can't work, it can't tell the reader anything unless he can accept the sophistry, the irony, the insincerity.

L.P. *Possibly you will make the reader feel that this is just one more piece of "show business." Irony cannot only protect truth. It can kill it too.*

J.H. But we can't protect the reader—that's not the aim. The reader doesn't want that. I think the reader wants to be let in on something, see something suddenly happen in the spontaneity that interviews are supposed to produce. Let's face it, the aim is very close to show business. Let's admit it: it's entertainment, isn't it? But what is entertainment really? It's a very serious, very important genre. The word *enter-tain* means "holding between": it's something that happens between the reader and us, it happens in fantasy, in imagination. Our fantasy of the reader and the reader's fantasies of us. Entertainment keeps this in-between world of fantasy, of imagination, of psyche alive, and happy, and well. An interview can be entertaining truth without being literally true, can't it? It can reveal us, show us, or be a show, without having to be show *business*. Only if this were business—and God knows it's costing us more than the reader—would it be suspect. I think the reader is not being cheated at all.

L.P. *Also there are all sorts of interviewers: Fallaci, David Frost, Cavett, Barbara Walters. Sometimes the interviewer can reach very far into things, like Socrates, and help, like a midwife.*

J.H. Are we supposed to be giving birth here? New raw red wet thoughts? No; no birthing, no midwifery—no psychoanalysis either.

L.P. *What's the difference?*

J.H. Maybe there isn't so much: after all, you are now the analyst, and I am doing my associating, letting come what comes.

L.P. *Still, there is a difference: The analyst does not want to know something from the patient; he just helps the patient to know what he or she doesn't know. An interviewer, however, does want to ask questions to get answers. So the interviewee is supposed to know answers: that's why he is being interviewed.*

J.H.   The main thing is that we both get out of the way. What can block the interview is "us," your thinking about what you have to get done here, and my thinking about my own thoughts, opinions, biography, myself. The "you" and the "me" can prevent the "inter." It's not *our* views that matter, it's the *"inter."*

L.P.   *You said that in an interview one is supposed to bring material evidence for his thought. You are supposed to be an expert and to win the agreement of your reader because of both your personality and your expertise. This belongs to the same domain as modern biographies. They try to impress, or argue, or convince. But wasn't it the same with classical dialogues and biographies?*

J.H.   Not at all! We cannot locate this interview in some classical model. It's not a classical dialogue as we just said, and it's not like classical biography either. A person who finishes reading an interview has just added more information to what he had before; he hasn't been changed by his reading as you might be by a Platonic dialogue. That moves your soul. It has a form. There is psychotherapy going on in those dialogues. How can an interview be therapeutic? The only form it might have is given by the length of the tape! The one biography I know that has this therapeutic effect is Jung's, and it has precious little "biographical detail," and so people say he didn't tell the truth. Biography is said to begin in Plutarch's *Lives*—that is the supposed modern source of what we mean by biography. But those figures of Plutarch's were an imaginal reconstruction of ideal types. He created fantasy figures. Or take the lives of the saints. These are transpersonal figures. The very fact that they were saints implied that they were divine in some way. They were ideal persons, persons beyond human persons, persons of the imaginal for the soul to "remember," to keep in touch with. . . . Maybe that's the archetypal impetus beyond biography: I mean trying to keep in touch with transpersonal, imaginal figures. Nowadays biography is a secular form; it's fallen, you might say. But I don't think the interview is really a fallen dialogue. It's altogether different. Those classical dialogues were never really spoken. We're dealing now with something spoken. And maybe the correct form of the interview is the tape. Because then there is the voice. And there is all the musical aspect of sound, the pauses. The great problem with the interview is that you lose the voice. You may pick up the speech pattern, the way the sentences are put together, but you lose the voice, you lose the crescendo, you lose the rhetorical aspect of all talk. You see, the big part of rhetoric, and we must talk about rhetoric, is that it's *spoken*. And it is the whole way you use your voice, in which is the body.

L.P. *It is also true that in an interview you cut off time.*

J.H. Yes, in an interview you have a destructive use of time. Why? You see, it seems in written work there are ways of building time into the writing. Through density, through descriptive passages, through changes of the patterns, through sudden moments of action which speed up the intensity of the plot, and then relaxations; there's a whole series of moves you can make in written work that can give the feeling of time. So that a person entering an old-fashioned novel feels he's left the world of time and entered the time of the story. And time stops, and you're lost in the book, and you hate when it ends because you have to come out again. There's a change of time in written work. An interview doesn't have the art that can produce a time, its own time. It's merely technically foreshortened or condensed, mathematically fifteen hours of taping into an hour and a half of reading. In other written work you can build time, you can replace the time in another way. And that time gives an echo to what's said. And without an echo to what's said there's no psyche, no psychology. So we have an interview about psychology, with a psychologist, without psyche in it. Unless we can get back the voice, the pauses, the echo, the sense of resonance or depth. There are moments when nothing happens except receptiveness, the mind going off in another direction. How can you put silence into an interview? Impossible.

L.P. *Nevertheless, here we are. What can we do?*

J.H. We must simply re-vision the interview. We've already gone through all the things we *don't* want to do. Why can't we make this a so-called interview, a deliteralized interview. After all, if we can do an interview that tries to re-vision the genre itself, then we are doing something more, something different than what we thought we were going to do. Then we have given value to the whole enterprise.

2 PATHOLOGIZING AND SOUL

L.P. *In most of your writings you have deliberately chosen the shadow aspects of the psyche: suicide, betrayal, masochism, masturbation, failure, depression, opportunism. But you never wrote on other shadow aspects like aggressivity, violence, power, sadism. Don't you find your attitude inconsistent?*

J.H. I don't try to be consistent. I don't even think about it. It would get systematic, everything fitting neatly. If you are really going to be polytheistic, you are bound—not to some principle of consistency—you are bound by the immediate necessity you are in. The psyche is very inconsistent—think of dreams. Consistency appears in dreams as *in*sistency, a return to the same place or person or agony insistently. . . .

L.P. *But why did you choose only passive, shadow aspects and leave out the active, aggressive ones?*

J.H. The things you mentioned—aggression, violence, power, sadism—aren't shadow at all; that's the whole Western ego! Go ahead, get ahead, do it. It's only when that breaks down, when depression comes in, and you can't get up and do it. When impotence happens and you can't get on with it. When you feel beaten, oppressed, knocked back . . . then something moves and you begin to feel yourself as a soul. You don't feel yourself as a soul when you're making it and doing it. So I've been concerned all along with those parts of behavior which, in our culture, further the sense of soul. This is not to say there isn't a huge question about violence and power and domination. But I can't attack violence and power and domination directly. I can go only where it begins to crumble, where the psyche itself undermines, and where fantasy begins to show. When you're in the middle of domination, you don't feel yourself in a *fantasy* of domination.

You are concerned with grabbing the object and getting what you want from it. But when you are suffering, when there's failure, dejection, and you are cast down, thrown back on yourself, left alone, wet, in one way or another—then you begin to feel, Who am I? What is going on? Why can't I? Why doesn't my will work? The Great Western Will—that I have been trained ever since I was a child to know what I want, to get it, and do it. To be independent! It doesn't matter whether you're a man or a woman here. You're taught to be independent, to stand on your own two feet, to take what you need, to know what you want, and to know where you're going. Now all of that gets defeated by the syndromes or the symptoms I'm talking about, the pathologizing. Suicide is one. Betrayal is one. Masturbation is another one, extremely important, because of the fantasy and the sense of oneself and the complications. But now, masturbation has become industrialized and it's . . .

L.P. *It's just pornography. . . .*

J.H. Well, not "just" pornography. I'm thinking of the equipment. It's a very large business. Even in upper-class department stores, there are "masturbation kits"—very clean, very plastic, well designed. Like home tools for your body. And the advertising for those machines—even if it doesn't use the word "masturbation"—talks about stress-relief, about relaxation, instead of excitement. Where's the secret, dirty excitement? Instead of surreptitiousness, we have workshops—probably about how to use the tools. It's become an anesthesia, like a tranquillizer that goes with watching TV. I think it once had fantasies in it: guilt, inhibitions, romance, images of all sorts. Strange images—postures and freakishness and longings and compulsive materials like Portnoy's liver. It was a rich psychological field that is now industrialized: all the fantasy is in the plastic equipment. It's the same way with depression. I think I said somewhere that the real revolution in our society begins with the person who can stand with his own depression. Because then you say no to the whole manic situation of modern society: overconsumption, overactivity, travel.

Here we sit in Zurich. You come up from Rome, I come over

from Texas. We never saw each other before. We sit down and start talking. That's manic. That's madness. We haven't written long letters to each other to know who the other is and what we feel and how we can talk, *if* we can talk. I haven't been on a boat for ten days crossing the ocean preparing. We assume we can at once talk, even talk significantly. That's manic! As if anyone can talk with anyone, which you can do on the telephone, of course, because there is no face, no eyes, no body there. The other is not taken into account on the telephone—just rude intrusions into someone's privacy. Manic. Our actual conversations are now modeled on telephone talk. No pauses, because if there is a moment of reflection, a moment of silence, you wonder if the other person is still there. Manic. Keep talking, like I'm doing now.

The culture expects one to be manic: hyperactive, spend and consume and waste, be very verbal, flow of ideas, don't stay too long with anything—the fear of being boring—and we lose the sense of sadness. For a good interview we have to move it. It can't really get stuck, repetitive, go down, dry up, let it affect us to the point where a conversation could affect us. The interview is supposed to be personal, but it's not supposed to enter the realm of depression. So the whole structure that you mentioned: aggressive, dominant, power, sadistic, we can also call manic. And that quality of the psyche is our ego development. It's so ego identified that we don't even see it as a syndrome! What we see as a syndrome is slowness, sadness, dryness, waiting. That we call depression, and we have a gigantic pharmaceutical industry to deal with it.

L.P. *It is usually thought that depression is the contrary of happiness, as masochism is the reversal of sadism. In your writings these nonactive phenomena become modes in their own right and are no longer the twisted mirror image of their contrary . . .*

J.H. You've touched on a very important point. If I look at a poem, I can't say that poem is the opposite of another poem. Or that this short story by Edgar Allan Poe is the opposite of a short story by D. H. Lawrence. It makes no sense. I have to work with the D. H. Lawrence story as it is. In the arts you don't use opposites. You may say there are strong contrasts in a painting, between blue and red or between the upper part and the lower part or the form and the content, whatever. But what's in front of the eyeballs, the image, isn't concerned with the question of opposites. I don't think about conscious versus unconscious or sadism versus masochism or activity versus passivity; I try to stick with what is presented.

There is another way I could go at this problem, which is through Christianity. The Christian view moves in on a situation immediately in terms of morality—good or bad; it starts off with a pair of opposites. So you're trapped in judgments before you examine the phenomenon. If you say activity is good, then passivity has to become negative and weak and neurotic. If passivity gets the plus sign, then activity has to become aggressive. You're caught. You can never deal with a thing as it is. So why not try to understand a phenomenon, darkness, say, without referring to light, without contrasting it with light. You can study the quality of the shadows, where they are, their thickness, their depth, whether these shadows are painted with purple or blue or umber or burnt umber or shades of gray, without any reference to light.

L.P. *But thinking in opposites seems unavoidable* . . . .

J.H. Yes, *thinking;* but feeling, perceiving, sensing, are not by means of opposites. Unfortunately, a lot of the thinking in psychology—either because it's Christian or because it's based on the law of contradiction or because it comes out of a certain kind of theoretical fascination with structure—is opposite. Even Freud and Jung have become "opposites" when they could be seen as brothers or as father and son.

I'm simply following the imagistic, the phenomenological way: take a thing for what it is and let it talk. And if we're talking about depression, let the depression show all the images of depression, whether it's saturnine depression or at the bottom of the sea with Dionysus or like Theseus sitting on a stone forever, heroic paralysis—so much to do, he can't move. Mars too has terrible depression: bitter lonely frustration, like rust; or Hera, "the left one" as she was called—forsaken, all alone, who cares? So many styles of depression . . . In the Middle Ages, for example, they had three animals that depicted depression: the pig, the dog, and the ass, I believe. But there is also the camel that can take the desert and the moose, alone in the woods, big and gangly and trying to hide. So, we had in the old lore of animals and of planets certain images of the depression. We didn't have to contrast depression with activity or with manic conditions. We don't have to see states as opposites.

L.P. *But then this is also true for masochism. Masochism has a world of its own. It is not only feminine, only passive, and the opposite of sadism: it is not only the passive response to an activity directed against it. Masochism is also a sort of destruction from the inside, like irony: one accepts the partner's rules so literally that they become nonsensical, absurd. One undermines them from the inside, in a sort of ironic mimicry. It shows the ritualistic, the compulsory, the mechanical side of any behavior like in a parody. In that sense masochism could be an ironic mode of reflection: and this is something that modern, contemporary theater shows very well.*

J.H. You need a certain masochism, a masochistic touch, for deepening—it is a mode of deepening into one's pain which is almost mystical. Which doesn't mean necessarily that one is in some way sadistic, or that there is a sadistic partner in it, and so on and so forth. How can you "undergo" or "submit"—those basic words for the process of psychological development—if you can't suffer? Awareness itself hurts. It isn't only a joy—there are joys when you suddenly see something or realize something—but there is also a painful aspect of going through analysis, whether you go actually into analysis or whether you just simply realize something. There is a feeling of pain involved in it. It hurts—that thought, that realization, that awareness. And that hurting is the same as becoming more sensitive. In English, "smart" means clever, intelligent, and it means sting, pain, hurt. Why does the psyche hurt us? Why does it have to hurt to realize something, to recognize something? Now, for me, that's a masochistic experience. There's a joy in that hurting because a layer of your skin's been peeled: you're that much more sensitive. Because the insight hurts and makes you more sensitive. You've got to be masochistic to become aware.

L.P. *So awareness is always connected with pain . . .*

J.H. Maybe that's why symptoms are so useful. And maybe, too, that's why I don't give much for the body-therapies—getting out all the kinks and tensions, relax, symptom-free. I feel masochism goes with consciousness . . . not get rid of the pain—after all, the psyche sends it, doesn't it?—but *enjoy* it, like a masochist. That's irony, though not quite what you meant by it, I guess.

L.P. *Your psychology is certainly not one of hedonism, of pleasure and joy.*

J.H. Let's not separate pleasure from pain in that abstract way, as if a serious depressive psychology didn't have its joy or its pleasures—for example, pleasures of the senses, pleasures of dwelling long and slow with things, pleasures of darkness. You see, for me, that's another aspect of the masochism of consciousness, it enjoys becoming conscious through pain. In the story of Eros and Psyche, Psyche suffers terrible torments and at the same time has a child in her belly called Voluptas and she works for Venus. Pleasure and pain are very complicated and very intertwined and psychology has pulled them apart into opposites. So we fear everything painful, missing the beauty and pleasure inside the very pain.

L.P. *But still you don't start from the joyous side; you seem always to begin where it hurts.*

J.H. I suppose I have a penchant for those conditions of failure, weakness, abandonment . . . But I think I can justify it theoretically. I mean we need to place this weakness, these pathologies into the theoretical fantasy of the Body, the Soul, and the Spirit. The soul is the middle ground in the traditions of Plato and Plotinus and Jung, too. The soul always seems to be weaker than or more "feminine" than or more receptive than the spirit. If you look at the language of the spirit, its descriptions, its images—it is always ultimate, absolute, high, the tops of the mountains; the soul is in the valley. In a piece I wrote called "Peaks and Vales," I touch on literature, religious texts, and common language, different places to contrast the phenomenology of the soul and the phenomenology of the spirit. The soul is experienced as something inferior.

There's a necessary inferiority when you're in psychic reality. One of the problems of this interview at the very beginning was how to do it, how do you stay psychological and yet be on top of everything—be on top—right there with the word, the logos. Logos, when working beautifully, leaves the soul out—if you bring the soul in, you start to stutter or you'll go around in circles or you'll be unable to elocute it in a way that does justice to it—you will be in half-darkness. My point is that soul means inferiority— something sensitive, something . . . well . . . pathologized. Soul makes the ego feel uncomfortable, uncertain, lost. And that lost-ness is a sign of soul. You couldn't have soul or be a soul if you couldn't feel that you have lost it. The person in the strong ego, as it's called, doesn't feel he's lost anything. That's one reason I question the psychiatric procedure of developing a strong ego. That seems to me a monstrous goal for psychotherapy because it attempts to overcome the sense of soul which appears as weak-ness, a weakness that seems almost to require symptoms. So these syndromes, these passive syndromes that you raised this question about, bring with them that feeling of inferiority. Violence or power or sadism or domination keep us from sensing soul, and until they crack from inside, don't work anymore, fall apart, as I have called it, we can't work with them. We have to concentrate on making soul out of the lost and inferior conditions.

L.P.   *We need to stop for a moment here. To an Italian audience, to an Italian subject, the very word "soul," anima, is repulsive, either because of the quality of inferiority inherent to the word, or because of the various layers of historical meanings deposited in it. To me it is strange to hear this word "anima" spoken by someone who is not a priest. It creates suspicion, resistances. "Psyche" is different: although the meaning is the same, it sounds more objective, it is not superstitious. The most common meaning of the word "anima" in Italian is a ghost . . .*

J.H.   What is the word in Italian for "self"?

L.P.   *"Sè."*

J.H.   *"Sè."* All right. And what is it in any other sense?

L.P.   *"Sè" is a reflexive pronoun.*

J.H. Reflexive. So you have the *"Io"* for "I" and the *"Sè,"* and "anima" for "soul."

L.P. *But "Sè" doesn't convey the same meaning as "self" in the Jungian sense.*

J.H. *"Sè"* doesn't have substance to it.

L.P. *No.*

J.H. I don't like those words *"Io"* and *"Sè"*—ego and self. They are subjectivist. Abstractions. Yet they seduce you into feeling they are real substantial entities. If only we could see them as personifications, as ghosts, as masks, as underworld entities. Now, "anima" does give that sense of soul beyond "me" as an ego and a self, beyond that subjective reflecting and subjective willing. When you use the word "anima" you know you are talking about a half-presence, a ghost kind of body.

As to the second part of your objection to the soul word, "anima"—I can't help. I can't help it if the Italians are still suffering from their Christian overload. It's partly your responsibility—if you didn't invent Christianity, at least you've kept it going a long time. Just because Christianity has ruined the word "anima" doesn't mean that it still can't evoke an ancient reality. Christianity took over a great deal of the old Latin language and theologized it. And it's the job of a psychological person today to reclaim psychology from theology where it has been trapped. The fact that theology made dogmas about the soul—about its immortality, about its nature, about the catechism, that the soul is divided into three parts, because Saint Augustine did this and this and this—doesn't necessarily mean that the individual today has to continue in that theological tradition. So soul-making—*fare anima* in Italian—is taking the soul out of jail. *Anima in carcere.* Taking the soul from the prison of theological concepts, the structures of consciousness which have oppressed the soul. Opening up that conceptual jailhouse—that's an Italian's job. The French have another job, and the Americans another job. The soul isn't given, it has to be made. And it has to be made out of the tradition you're in. And one way or another, you're going to have to fight or struggle or peel away the wrappings in which it's been culturally trapped. Even though an Italian hears the word "ani-ma" through a *deformation théologique,* this doesn't mean we shouldn't use that word. The word "anima" and the implications of it are far richer than what happened to it through theological oppression.

You said something else about why one doesn't like the word: it evokes weakness, inferiority? Is that it? Well, that's exactly what it's supposed to do! It's supposed to evoke weakness. I use "anima" to evoke something different than *"Io."* And the image of the *Io,* the ego, is strength; it should be strong, healthy and active, firm—you know, all those robust muscle things. But "ani-ma" has that sense of weakness—what is so threatening about that?

L.P. *Lameness. Harmlessness. . . .*

J.H. Harmlessness. Weakness. Hopelessness. Dependency? The descriptions that you are using—that language—is exactly the ex-perience. Moodiness, too, perhaps. Well, that's exactly how Jung describes anima as a psychic component. Anima makes a person sensitive, moody, bitchy, a little bit helpless, a little bit uncertain. And when you work with those conditions you become psycho-logical: you discover interiority, you become reflective, you notice your own atmosphere. So the resistance to the anima is also a resistance to the psychological. It's a resistance on the part of an omnipotence-fantasy ego . . . to crafting or shaping or working with those conditions of softness, uncertainty. Imagination is in that. The Renaissance writers—and I think now of *Letters* by Pe-trarch, *Letters* by Ficino, *Letters* by Michelangelo—are filled with anima: depression, weakness, sickness, complaint, love of differ-ent kinds, helplessness. They aren't able to do what they want to do. Of course, these men were extremely active: Ficino never stopped his work despite all his complaints about being para-lyzed and being unable to do anything anymore. Michelangelo thought he was old when he was forty and then he went on living beyond eighty. The soul builds its endurance, its "stamina" as Rafael Lopez calls it, through hopelessness and depression. I think the Italians have an enormous sense of anima, just because they know immediately what its moods feel like. It's only that you needn't take all those moods and all those weaknesses and helplessnesses and so on as literal. One thing you do learn in therapy is how, when you have a depression, it belongs to you, but you don't identify with the mood. You live your life in the depression. You work with the depression. It doesn't completely stop you. It only stops you if you're manic. Depression is worst when we try to climb out of it, get on top of it.

L.P. *You are suggesting that all the syndromes you mentioned are not depressive or pathological . . .*

J.H. No, no. I don't deny syndromes, I don't whitewash pathology. But we have to look at psychopathology from the psyche's viewpoint. Syndromes simply manifest the pathologizing process—the soul does this to us, and we have to start with that fact and not with our ego illusions about how we "ought" to be. Syndromes make our ideas very, very real. We talk about love, say, but when we get jealous, paranoidly, impossibly jealous, then the syndrome brings love home to us in a very powerful way.

Say you have an idea like *"festina lente"* [hasten slowly], or Petrarch's idea of "looking backward in order to see forward." It is an ideal, a piece of wisdom, or a motto to inscribe on a personal book marker. I saw *"festina lente"* carved in stone on a building at Yale. It becomes an objectified idea: "Hey, wouldn't it be wonderful to move forward by looking backward; to move quickly slowly, to make haste slowly." So, then I put the idea into practice: I tell myself, "Take it easy, don't move so fast." Or when I'm just wasting time, I tell myself, "That's all right, I can be moving slowly, slowly." The objectified idea has become a prescription, a piece of cheap wisdom or a superego command. They become programs. Moralisms. But to take these Renaissance maxims *psychologically* would be to recognize that the psyche itself works according to these dictums. *Festina lente* is then experienced like a symptom, it's going on in your actual behavior when you find yourself moving forward quickly in a conversation and losing the thread, forgetting what you wanted to say, which is happening now in this interview. That is already *festina lente* working; stopping our forward movement and yet hastening it too. The psyche itself double binds us. These Renaissance maxims weren't preached from the pulpit of the ego—they were digestives, they were re-gurgitations ... epitomes of how the psyche actually behaves.

L.P. *I am still thinking about weakness, that the soul makes us weak. You said you can feel weak without having to be weak. That would be staying with the soul's mood without taking it into the ego, the Io as an identification.*

J.H. That's one of the first things you learn in therapy, isn't it?

L.P. *No. I think you first learn to feel what you feel, thoroughly.*

J.H. To feel something thoroughly does not mean to be it thoroughly. It is a mistake, a big bad mistake, to take feelings utterly literally. Psychotherapy has got itself caught in this worship of feelings. If we took ideas that literally, we would say a person was paranoid, but we take feelings as if they were the truth of who and what we are. Look, when you get depressed, it belongs to you and you can't help but feel it thoroughly (unless you take pills or go into a manic defense), but you don't have to be identified with the mood. You can live your day in a depressed style. Things slow down, there is a lot of sadness. You can't see over the horizon. But you can notice all this, recognize it, and go on—my God, thousands of people live like this, regularly or in periods. You can find ways of talking from it, seeing the world through it, connecting to people without covering it. It's amazing how others can respond to your depression *if you don't identify with it:* a sigh immediately produces a sigh in the other person. Did you ever think what a relief to be with someone who knows how to live in the depression without being it. That's a master to learn from, like old people sometimes can be. Depression lets you live down at the bottom. And to live down at the bottom means giving up the Christian thing about resurrection and coming out of it; "light at the end of the tunnel." No light fantasy; and then the depression at once becomes less dark. No hope, no despair. That message of hope only makes hopelessness darker. It's the greatest instigator of the pharma industry ever!

Notice how often, when we work on something, anything, we have to go back. Or a thought comes up later on, afterward. You have to go all the way back to something that happened a few days ago and look back on that thought in order to move forward in that thought. Now those slow rings are psychological behaviors that happen automatically. What we think are—what the ego would think are—symptoms, losing the thread, repeating, regressing, reiterating, going back, *esprit d'escalier,* all of those things are actually modes in which this peculiar behavior of the psyche works.

L.P. *It is the same as the meter, rhythm, and rhyme in poetry: the same pattern returning all the time, like a rhythm, that gives the poem its particular, individual time and keeps the sequence or words and meaning going. It also determines the meaning: it is a shape, a form that helps—not only helps but contains. . . .*

J.H. Exactly. It helps and contains. And all the art forms have those abstract cultural modes for both containing and preventing a direct, one-sided linear motion. That's what keeps, I would guess, the art forms psychological; they speak to the soul, when I say psychological.

L.P. *But this repetitive mode is also the mode of compulsions and obsessions. . . .*

J.H. I guess the difference there with the *"ossessione,"* the obsessional part, is if that repetition, that rhythm doesn't deepen by return, if it doesn't turn by return, if it doesn't revision, or echo, then there is something merely obsessional. But the obsession is an attempt to get to that deepening. To rework it again. If you watch anyone doing handwork, it's all obsessional. You can't make lace without an obsession. You can't turn a pot. Art has that constant fussing with the same little place. Now that's exactly what we all do with a symptom. We keep going back and fussing with it. You are jealous, and you go back fussing and fussing over a little suspicion, working it over a thousand times. The obsessive jealous thought can also be seen as a way of making something happen. It isn't just "working it through" as the psychoanalysts say: actually, you may be making something out of it, making something up, making a fiction, an imagination, and the fussing in jealousy can be polishing the image, so to speak. Let's say your wife or your lover gives you a suspicion that there is another person ... and you begin to ask every possible sort of question, trying to get all sorts of details, sexual details. Your mind is utterly obsessed with getting the image of the other person, the scene, rubbing it, polishing it, getting a fantasy going. It's a kind of imaginational voyeurism. Here's where you need Balzac or Proust or Stendahl—where you need some background to this pathologizing, so you can see what force for imagination these jealousy events have. This doesn't mean you will write novels. It doesn't even mean that the pathologizing is going to stop when it is fully talked out and "understood." I have yet to "understand" jealousy, except as I am now talking about it. I am trying to follow what the psyche itself does with these paranoid obsessive questions. A demand for details, precision. To get the image precise by worrying it, by going over it a thousand times. It's extraordinary what a fever pitch of imagining starts. You would think you wouldn't want to know the details. And yet the psyche constructs, like a jeweller, a watchmaker, in this obsessional way. It's making an image of the event.

L.P. *Then, when does the pathology come in?*

J.H. It doesn't come in, it's there all the time! The pathology is the place that keeps the person *in* the soul, that torment, that twist that you can't simply be naive, you can't simply go along in a natural way, that there's something broken, twisted, hurting, that forces constant reflection—and work, in Bachelard's sense. There's a work going on all the time, a fire burning, there's something *elemental* happening. The analyst coming at therapy with a medical background sees the pathologies within a medical framework and has to deal with them as medical problems to be cured or healed or treated. If you come at the pathology from a psychological perspective, then you're dealing with pathology in terms of the soul's way of working on itself. Then the pathology, I think, is necessary to that working of imagination.

L.P. *Do you think it necessary to be insane in order to become psychological? An approach to psyche through madness?*

J.H. No. That doesn't mean that a person should be so pathologized that he can do nothing except his compulsions or so pathologized that he can do nothing but be in a paranoid delusion, psychotically pathological, chronically pathological, so it becomes utterly determining and nothing else can happen. That part of the pathology is always a mystery, no one has the answer to why the human being gets stuck this way. The Buddha didn't know, and psychiatry doesn't know, and we don't know what madness is. But we do know that in a usual person who comes to therapy there is a torment of some kind, a pathology of some kind. And the first move is to affirm it—not fight it or even analyze it. Give the pathology shelter. Let it sit down in the chair.

L.P. *In some of your works you used the word "pathology" to qualify psychotic situations, and you used these situations as enactments of some myth. So, this way myth comes into the therapeutic scenario. On the other hand, when you talk about pathology in your therapeutic practice it seems to be obvious that you are talking about what is usually called neurotic symptoms. . . . How can you work out this contradiction or do you think it is a contradiction?*

J.H. First of all psychosis and myth don't necessarily go together, even though you find that idea in Jung. It's not my idea that you see myth best in psychosis. I think mythological behavior is going on all the time. The doctor is in a myth, too, even if differently than the patient. Mythological behavior doesn't mean that you walk around like a God; mythological behavior means that you are behaving with the rhetoric of a certain style, whether you are in Apollonic consciousness or you're in Saturnian consciousness or you're acting the Great Mother or whatever. You can be a perfect "normal," a normal married woman with three bambini and doing everything right, driving your minicar . . . dressing for every occasion . . . never missing a Mass, and you can be in Hera consciousness. The myth is going on right there. It isn't a matter of being crazy to be mythical. That is a romantic perversion! So I don't mean that at all about psychosis and myth, to begin with.

Psychosis is mostly boring, narrow. It's not that rich, wild field people tend to believe it is; it's actually more of an impoverishment, and rigid, too. Even a florid manic phase hasn't the wealth of contents you might suppose. The firecrackers aren't that dazzling. What makes a psychotic condition interesting isn't the psychosis, it's *who* has the psychosis; what is the nature, the character of that particular psyche. Maybe, though, I just haven't the ability with psychosis that some analysts may have. Maybe I'm too defended against psychosis to be good at working with it. I have nothing "against it," you know, it's that I'm more concerned with the normal sort of craziness—and the craziness called "normality." I'm interested in the fear of it you have and I have and the expressions of it in daily life where it is disguised or acceptable or how we find ways of handling it in religion or addiction or sexuality or business or traveling or eating. Politics, too. I mean craziness is all around us—not merely as it is narrowed and literalized in the "crazy population" in asylums, in the drugged patients and statistically reported patients and sociologically analyzed.

L.P. *So you are trying to break down the classification between psychotic and neurotic?*

J.H. And normal. I don't find the terms that useful. I am as afraid of normal people as I am of psychotics. More even of "normals"—because of the repression. It's the neurotics, as we tend to call them, I am most at home with. And then, you left out another group: psychopaths—are they normals? I tend to think so—at least in our culture. . . . But we are going off the track.

L.P. *Are there certain mythical patterns or specific Gods who are more healthy, let us say, for our lives and other Gods who are more pathological? Your own writings seem to have favored Dionysus, Hermes, and Pan and Hades, while you have been attacking Apollo, especially, as far back as* Suicide and the Soul.

J.H. Apollo certainly presents a pattern that is disastrous, destructive for psychological life, cut off from everything that has to do with feminine ways, whether Cassandra or Creusa or Daphne—whomever he touches goes wrong—so that you have the feeling that Apollo simply doesn't belong where there is psyche. But then, another moment comes along where the Apollonic is utterly essential, for example, when you need form, when you need distance, when you need an ideal image for orientation. Sometimes the soul needs discipline and wants sunshine, clear and distinct ideas. If you resist Apollo completely, consistently, then he can't come in and there is no sense of form, no clarity, no prophetic deeper insight. You are always confusing everybody and keeping things emotional. There's no detachment, not even from the waiter in the restaurant, from the car in front of you— it's all involvement all day long. Or, Apollo gets you from behind: you become pure and rigid about your involvements: they become Apollonic principles, ideals.

L.P. *If all the gods have their styles of pathologizing, then the only possible path of psychological health is to be aware of all of them. Isn't that too much to expect?*

J.H. It's not a matter of trying to make a place for all the Gods like a circus manager with three rings, a place for them all at once, the Twins on the high-wire, Hercules lifting weights, and Dionysus among the panthers. You aren't a manager anyway— even Zeus can't really manage the Gods. It's more a matter of realizing appropriateness, what Plato called fittingness, a sense of what is happening now and how it fits in, and which God, just now, has been neglected, and in which way neglected. Psychological health, if you like, doesn't start with a principle. It is a sensitivity. A recognition.

L.P. *Still, you use the image of the circus manager, and even if you say one isn't the manager, don't you imply nevertheless, that you, the human person, do invite in or exclude this or that God and by doing so, invite in or exclude this or that style or pathologizing?*

J.H. We are entangled in their myths—we can't exclude them. The soul lives mythically: it may be inside us, but it is also inside the Gods—and that's the more significant way to imagine the soul: as being entangled in myths, as being inside the Gods. So, we are always going to get into their styles of destructiveness— cheating like Hermes and tricking. Think of what Dionysus did to Pentheus! Think of sweet beautiful golden Venus and what she did to Hippolytus and Phaedra or the whole Trojan war. There's no way out. And that sense, that feeling of being bound by their necessity, turns us toward them. I don't see how we can ever realize the soul as *real*, and that mythical things really are happening to us, except through pathologies.

3 PSYCHOANALYSIS AND SCHOOLS

L.P. *In your book* The Myth of Analysis *you wrote that Freud behaved like the founder of a religion, or a sect. You are a Jungian who has stepped out from Jungian orthodoxy and founded a new school, archetypal psychology. Don't you think you are in the same myth in which Freud was, the myth of the founder?*

J.H. No. Not a founder in that sense. My way of working is to take something already in place and twisting it, turning it, give it your own turn. They say about Bach, "He left no form as he found it," and what I want to do with Jung or with Freud is to leave no form as I found it. Therefore, people say I'm twisting Jung—I think that the spirit in Jung's work gets another shape each time you pick it up, and different people pick it up differently. I picked it up my way. Some have never put their own hands on it, really . . . they have played it back like a gramophone. Without Jung I would not have been able to think any of the things I thought. Pupils make a founder. Pupils take you literally and turn you into a founder. They take your thought and write theses about it, explanations, interpretations, and they want to practice it according to rules; they read what you said and they say, "That is what *he* said and I am going to do it that way"; and they stop twisting it!

L.P. *So you are neither a pupil of Jung nor a heretic; nor are you an individual thinker since you say you are simply "twisting" Jung or Freud. What then do you consider yourself to be?*

J.H. This twisting may be the way to be both a Jungian and an individual thinker. At least that's how I imagine what I do. I am blamed for not being independent enough. . . .Why do I hide behind the mask of being a Jungian, why don't I call my school what it is, why do I always say, "I'm just working further from

Jung's thought"? Either you start being one of them or get out! But I don't think that's the way to do it. My tradition is more Jewish: you stay in the *schul* and you write a commentary below the line, you just go on commenting, and you add a new midrash on the text, and your originality is in the midrash. If you stay in the depth psychological tradition, then you stay as an Adlerian, a Jungian, Freudian, and you go on doing what they did, departing from, breaking with, commenting on, reacting to each other. They did their original thinking within the same terrain, that's the way I want to do it. *And,* this is very important—they did *not* integrate each other (though Jung claims he does with his type theory). They were not eclectics: taking a bit of this and a bit of that, like supermarket shopping or something. Eclecticism is the devil. It's better to be a Jesuit, very, very strict for a long time and think your way through. Descartes, you know, went to a Jesuit school, and he thought his way out, at least partly.

L.P.   *Your midrash fantasy doesn't feel convincing. For instance, I didn't come here because you are a commentator. You have taken new steps, opened new perspectives that are original enough for me to want to do this interview, and there is a public, readers, who want to hear what you have to say. You are quoted, invited to speak. You have a following and pupils: they buy your books, they travel to hear your lectures, they come to your seminars and to your practice, and they write about archetypal psychology— like this interview.*

J.H.   Well, there is another fantasy besides the commentator one which was, anyway, in regard to Jung and Freud, how I view myself relative to the traditional schools. But as to followers, as you call them, the fantasy is more that I feel myself a member of a body, a community . . . a kinship with people who work with similar ideas or at least are trying to re-vision things. It can be therapy, it can be philosophy, it can be religion. It can be in criticism or classics and mythology. These people are not followers, not "my students"—they're often way ahead of me. Some are even older than me. And I doubt if psychology is their main focus. They are friends . . . there is nothing else to call them. Friends. We are all sort of in love with each other. There's an emotion, an intensity, even though we are spread all over everywhere. It's an active demonstration of what Alfred Adler called *Gemeinschaftsgefühl,* fellow feeling.

L.P. *But this fellow feeling is not with Jungians?*

J.H. Oh, quite a few are Jungian analysts, formally trained and very active. But many others aren't at all. It's very loose, they're very independent, and we don't collaborate directly—we stimulate one another, indirectly. Sometimes we meet at a conference or do a summer school together or meet at a special thing like the lecture in Florence. It's more like a community—*Gemeinschaft*—there's no organization nor officials. The basis of our connection is ideas not organization . . . an erotic connection through ideas. This erotic basis also takes care of those arguments about priority, giving credit or taking credit for an idea. The ideas themselves are communal . . . nobody owns them, so we borrow and steal from each other all the time . . . no "fear of influence" . . . people use what I write without quoting me directly. That's what ideas are for—to be used, and who says they are "mine"?

The same is true with me: I take all sorts of things from conversations with these friends, things from my wife, and I put them in "my" books. My wife has always been very important to all this. So far none of us has staked out claims and had fights. Everybody seems very generous—or better, everybody feels the community—at least that's my fantasy about it. We are all glad to see each other. We play baseball and we dance and talk and shout, and we listen. We listen to each other. It's a marvelous thing, and I feel as much pride in this way of living a school of ideas as in the ideas themselves. It gives each of us an imaginary community in which the others are all figures. It ties your thoughts to an imaginary loving audience and feeds your thoughts when you sit alone. You imagine them and feel their interest. You see, if we were organized into a real school, or a movement, all this would become literal and the eros would go, and we would have an institution in its place. I used to want a community—all of us at the same university—but a community doesn't have to live all in the same place . . . that can be a mistake for intellectual work. Too much time is spent organizing things. One has to keep the community semi-imaginal . . . like the letter-writing communities: Petrarch, Ficino, and probably the romantics, too.

L.P. *You say that your community demonstrates Adler's* Gemeinschaftsgefühl *and you discussed this notion of community in both your article in the* Enciclopedia Italiana *and in your 1977 lecture at Eranos. What you describe demonstrates the central place you put the myth of Eros and Psyche. For you psychology is an erotic phenomenon. Although you do not write directly about eros except in certain essays, there is passion, emotion, and an erotic attitude toward the psyche all through your work. In your community of friends, however, it seems the eros is of a particular kind: it requires separation and mobility, it requires ideas, and it requires no worldly organization. This seems an eros of the puer archetype: unattached and inspirational.*

J.H. That we live in different places and work in different fields avoids the power problems that get into a community when it becomes a school. We are not in competition with each other. We are not all psychologists . . . our focus is not narrow—it's multiple, let's say, a polytheistic community. The senex part appears in our loyalty and our seriousness and our diligence. Everybody works very hard. But it doesn't appear in the need for a unified organization or even a club. The main thing, though, is not the actual presence of each other . . . it's the imaginal presence: puer eros, you call it. I think as we die off, we will still remain present as figures for those who are left.

L.P. *I'd like to get clearer about your relation to the Jungian school. You said you are both a Jungian and independent of it. Can you clarify where your ideas are Jungian and where not?*

J.H. Some of it already shows in what's written. For instance, I don't emphasize, or even use, some of Jung's terms, like: self, compensation, opposites, types, psychic energy. You won't find anything about mandalas and wholeness, and I don't refer much to Eastern thought, synchronicity, and the Judeo-Christian God-image. My favorite books are not *Aion* and *Answer to Job*. When I use the term "ego," I put ironic marks around it: the so-called ego, because for me the task of psychology is to see through it and get around it. I certainly don't place this construct, ego, in the center of consciousness. Then, Jung was always fascinated by psychosis . . . schizophrenia . . . and he looked at people and psychic contents in terms of latent psychosis. Jung also had a science-side—physics, the association experiment, parapsychology. He even did some astrological statistics. But you know what's in his *Collected Works.*

L.P. *Is your divergence, then, in regard to basic concepts and emphasis?*

J.H. It's more a shift in, or a kind of, consciousness. I think today we are just less literal.

L.P. *Most of the usual criticism of Jung and his school centers around its lack of published cases, what you might call empirical evidence, and on the lack of a specific theory of the different kinds of neuroses. Jung is also criticized for neglecting language and semantics, the arts—and philosophy, for example, his contemporary, Heidegger.*

J.H. People expect so much! From one man. Why should he be blamed for what he didn't do? If he leaves out something, like Heidegger, he probably had good reason. It wasn't his job. If he doesn't spell out a special theory of neurosis like the Freudians, it shows he questions the value of that whole way of thought. It would have been a waste of his time.

L.P. *Your adherence to the Jung school seems to lie in sharing the same omissions. You both leave out the same kind of things—more or less. What, then, makes you a Jungian in a positive sense?*

J.H. His psychological attitude. He really does start in the soul— *esse in anima.* And the scope, the freedom of his mind. The wealth. His *chutzpah*—to take on anything, the entire cultural problem in which the modern person is set. His running engagement with Christianity. He really did struggle with the curse of Christianity. His sense of collective outer events bearing in on one—like Christianity, like racial roots, like geography, like ancestors. His attitude toward the *diamones* and powers, active imagination and talking with the little people, and his subtlety about myths and how the psyche and therapy are mythical. He opened up the psyche as a field of images . . . and psychotherapy for him is alchemical, archetypal—not personal, not reductive. I think of therapy, of the psyche, alchemically, and this comes straight from Jung. . . . You know Jung's whole last part of his life was in alchemy, but his followers—with only a few rare exceptions—don't touch it. They are still doing types, parents, and ego psychology. I think very much in terms of shadow and anima and animus. . . .

But after saying all that, I have to make a distinction again. For instance, Jung worked out of the old wise man of nature, and he read things, dreams, for instance, prophetically. I don't at all. I have more aesthetic and urban attitudes, so I use cultural reflections. He didn't like high culture, and he really didn't like neurotic modern "unnatural man" and prefers to reflect in terms of tribal people, peasant people. But maybe one of the biggest differences is that I tend to use "imagination" instead of that word "unconscious" . . . not that there isn't unconsciousness in us all the time . . . but I won't use the word as an abstract noun to cover over the cultural implications that are in imagination. Jung takes the unconscious as a field of nature. It still bears traces of Freud's id, Darwinian prehistorical islands or Africa. Besides, the word "unconscious" is loaded with subjectivity and has become a psychologism. "Imagination" connects you at once with a tradition and with aesthetic activity. With language. It refers directly to images which Jung himself says are the main content of the unconscious.

L.P. *"Unconscious" also means the seat of conflicts that are repressed and the habits and desires of the child in one.*

J.H. Certainly. But if we re-vision the idea of unconscious as imagination, then we will look at, we will imagine, the child differently and also the conflicts differently. My childish habits and desires are not only things that have to "grow up" and "adapt to reality," they're not only potentials for growth or creativity, and they're not only the places I need for regression, ways of protecting myself when I feel low and small. Those habits belong to an archetypal child, too, and that child is crucial to my survival as a man of fantasy, to the survival of my imagining capacity, and that's tied to my weakness, my dependency, or what psychology calls my childishness. So you see, all these ideas we are so used to, like the unconscious and repressed childishness, need to be re-visioned.

L.P. *The Jungian school must have a great deal of difficulty with you since you are so clearly Jungian in your attitude, in your spirit, in your close involvement with Jung's work, and yet you are not Jungian conceptually, "to the letter." You don't take Jung literally—and that could put you outside the Jung school, since schools require a literalism and a belief.*

J.H. That's not how I work with ideas. I don't "believe" Jung or "believe in" his ideas. His ideas are valuable because they are so good to work with and against. Good ideas, like Jung's, allow the widest play for thought.

M.B. *You know that Jung supposedly said at the end of his life that he stood for everything he ever wrote. Would you say you believed in your ideas, your own work?*

J.H. What difference would it make to make a pronouncement of belief of that sort? Does a dog believe in his bone? Of course, while he is chewing it. But ask him Dog, do you believe in your bone? He'll growl. A cat will just walk away from you—and the bone too. The cat doesn't care about believing.

L.P. *You would have to believe in your own "school" to set up your own school.*

J.H. To set up a school creates immediately a new orthodoxy. We certainly don't need more orthodoxies—if anything, we need more heterodoxies. Not even that: doxies are opinion, that's what the word means. Beliefs are simply strong opinions. So, no beliefs, no schools; no orthodoxies, no heterodoxies. Let's just go on with the bones.

L.P. *There's also a material aspect in schools. The fact that a psychoanalytical sect guarantees patients and clients. So it's also an economical structure.*

J.H. Oh, it's more than an economical structure; it's got all the corruption of an economical structure. As long as the school perpetuates itself through its rituals of training "requirements," then it becomes a necessity for the "senior" analysts to go on with that training, to train others, and half or even ninety percent of their practice is no longer therapeutic practice, it's training practice. . . . To be a training analyst is to be an apparatchik. The candidate is buying a good investment for his future, like insurance, so he doesn't object. And the training analyst is selling insurance, and indulgences: passports to the self.

L.P. *It's self-reproductive. . . .*

J.H. Yes, self-reproductive at regular fees. So once you set up a training institute you set up that form of corruption as well. It doesn't *intend* to be corrupt. It just happens out of the institutional necessity of the school. The analysts have to live, and if their patients happen to be candidates they live off their candidates. We need more analysis, more psychology of institutions and economics. Psychology has taken these things over as impersonal objective forms, without realizing that they too have an unconscious imagination. There's a depth psychology that affects each person in an institution. I'm very wary of doing training because of that unconscious imagination in the institution itself. It's immensely powerful. A university isn't just a place, and a school isn't just a building. It's a collective system with its own systematic unconsciousness which makes each person in the school unconscious in a collective way, and usually about the institution itself. Haven't you noticed how people in a church or a hospital or a business are always analyzing it, trying to become conscious about what they are in. That's what I mean by corruption in training institutes: getting caught in a terrible unconsciousness, all the while pretending to be developing consciousness and guiding soul. It's not that I'm clean and uncorrupt or holy. I've done training. I've been in institutions. It's just that I'm wary. I don't know how to keep the eros alive in an institution.

L.P. *You were talking previously about the role of tradition in the Jungian school. Tradition can also be experienced as a very strong inhibiting factor, a burden, especially in regard to the Jungian school.*

J.H.   A curious thing is that there's never been a single piece of true doctrinal dispute, theoretical dispute, among the Jungians. They fight bitterly over rules and over personalities, but the odd thing is that they do not take ideas that seriously.

L.P.   *Why do you think the Jungians have this sort of general agreement or commitment not to fight over ideas, or is it something inherent to the Jungian style of thought?*

J.H.   It seems inherent, because Jung himself was not very concerned with critically revising his own thought. Of course he "broke with Freud," as they say, and "founded his own school," but when he revises his thought, it is to turn against Freud's—not his own thought—of the time. He just rewrites the chapter or the book and leaves out certain paragraphs, puts in new thoughts; he gives it a new cast, like repainting a picture, but he doesn't find his arguments need to be overtly, literally, explicitly corrected. Freud does. Freud says, "Back in so-and-so I thought that the libido was derived all from the id, but since then I found that there's an ego instinct, and so on. . . . I've had to correct my libido theory. . . ." He's constantly making theoretical revisions. It seems to me Jung is thinking more as a person of imagination. Imagination does not argue and does not correct itself, it just plays a new tune. One piece of music, a mazurka, does not criticize or refute a sonata. Now, Freud thought he was writing a kind of scientific psychology, so he found contradictions in what he wrote and those contradictions had to be settled one way or another to advance the theory, as you would if you were doing physics or physiology or something like that. Jung and the Jungians allow the different modes of their imagination to develop without seeing that as contradiction. That answers your question, positively, kindly.

L.P.   *And if we look at it less generously?*

J.H.   From another viewpoint, it seems that Jungians are not interested in ideas. Many Jungians have the feeling they have all the ideas they need; Jung gave them the ideas, all they need do is apply them or work with them. They are satisfied. Oh, you are getting to me now. . . . I can feel my gorge rising: "the Jungians" are one monstrous complex for me; I am one of them and so I can't bear them—except for some good personal friends. Sometimes I suppose it's because they don't all think like I think, so I am enraged because I am vain. Other times I think, they really are mostly second rate people with third rate minds. Still other times—and it is interesting, isn't it, how an interview can bring all this up, the interview as therapeutic hour—I feel the terrible *versagen*, cop-out, *mauvaise foi*, the failure to carry on and carry further what Jung gave them. They simply live off Jung's ideas (or Freud's, for that matter) without working the field one inch further themselves. This is a gigantic betrayal, a dishonesty. You must pay for what you get from a school by working those ideas further. All they care about are training qualifications—keeping others out of their union. And, it's all couched in pseudomysticism about individuation and wholeness.

L.P. *What would be "working the field further themselves"?*

J.H. Not every one is a writer. I don't mean writing. I don't mean research in amplification either, though at least that would be something. I surely don't simply mean practicing. First, it would be to inquire, to doubt everything they are sure of and rest on, to let themselves be challenged, to risk themselves in public. Therapy is a cushion: and not just for the patient. The analyst, as Thomas Szasz says, is the only professional who cannot be challenged. A lawyer has an opposing lawyer and judge who watches. A surgeon operates under the eyes of colleagues and nurses. Even a banker has "controls." But the only person, besides the analyst, who knows what goes on in analysis, Szasz says, is the patient and he is disqualified from the beginning because the patient is "only a patient," incompetent by definition.

L.P. *You do get terribly angry about all this. And not just about Jungians, about psychotherapy itself. Why then do you practice it?*

J.H. I am amazed by the psyche. I love to work it. I do this and that all day—write, edit, pay bills, cook, rush around tending to life, have my siesta and tea and then late afternoon and evening come and practice begins. What a pleasure to get in the chair and receive the imagination and imagine with it and have that back and forth of dismantling, insighting, fantasying, exposing, pressing forward. It's tiresome, too, of course, when there are other things on the mind. But that's rarely. I'm not a terribly good listener usually. I go to a party or a meeting and hear all sorts of things, and when I tell my wife it's usually only what *I* said that I remember. But in analysis, amazingly enough, I concentrate the whole time, I listen, I remember. I recall images and dreams from years before that a patient had. It's a natural joy for me.

L.P.   *So you do it because you like to do it?*

J.H.   That's certainly one answer.

L.P.   *Don't you want to help people?*

J.H.   Sure, but it's irrelevant. I can't help people directly. Only the psyche can, so I try to help the psyche or serve it; *therapeia.* And working on psychological ideas is part of that *therapeia.*

L.P.   *The ideas that psychotherapy has produced about psychotherapy—and I am thinking now of British writers like Winnicott and Fairbairn and the Tavistock group and object relations theory or American writers like Searles or Kohut—do not enter your writings. Why not?*

J.H.   They block my imagination ... even Winnicott who writes about imagination and playing. These writings are too conceptual, they are written in an explanatory, scientific style, they are Freudian—not in content, but Freudian in style. Stylistically, I'm a Jungian. We all know, since Alfred Adler, that psychodynamic explanations are fictions, but these other schools you mentioned take these fictions as psychodynamic explanations. And then there is no breadth of culture, of imagery, in their writings. Take Kohut for instance—those thick books on narcissism, but where is Narcissus, the beautiful boy, the pond, and Echo flitting about and the drowning. The beauty is missing. I appreciate the finesse of their observations, the moves they make in therapy, but I just can't read their psychodynamic language.

L.P. *This may be your most fundamental difference with all schools and also your main originality: you do not accept psychodynamics.*

J.H. I am not so sure it's so original. Physicists, theologians, Zen teachers—all said the map is not the territory. Psychologists seem not to have learned that. All these explanations of human life are for me fictions, fantasies. I like to engage them on that level, but only as fictions, as archetypal fantasies. They may have therapeutic value, like any story can have. They may help the therapist get a second-level structure, an ordering grid while he is in the middle of the confusion. But psychodynamics—and I don't care whether role-playing theories, infantile development theories, or the Gods themselves—keeps us in explanations. We cannot explain the psyche. We are the psyche. The soul wants imaginative responses that move it, delight it, deepen it . . . explanatory responses just put us back into positivism and science—or worse, into delusion, a kind of *maya* or *avidya,* an ignorance that makes us believe we know. You notice that one after another these explanations excite us and then fail. Kohut is just the latest in a line of delusions that the mind grids itself on. And always that hope for redemption. Let the grid go. Instead of trying to explain human behavior let's try to see through the fantasy of explanation. The grids, the systems don't even serve as support systems for the therapists. They are screens for keeping out the images and figures who might really tell them something interesting.

L.P. *What about your own grids, those that your pupils take from your work and apply as archetypal psychology?*

J.H. Terrible. . . . It all starts with the idea of "a school." If only school could go back to *skole*, what it first meant, "leisure," a kind of entertainment, maybe. If only pupils could *entertain* ideas. That's all; that's enough, because the mind is moved by entertaining ideas more than by using them, laying them out, outside the mind, in applications. A few years ago I was so bothered by everyone using archetypal psychology . . . ughh—that term itself, and "soul-making" and "the imaginal" and referring to Gods—that I began a little book called "Why I Don't Read

Hillman." I collected all the objections people had to what I was doing. I made notes on all the dodges in my own thinking, all the loopholes and cover-ups—everything I couldn't bear in my own work.

L.P. *Where is that now?*

J.H. Well . . . I like to think it's in the newer work, that is, incorporated in what I try to do as I do it rather than having to write a separate tract, like Augustine's *Retractions*.

L.P. *Your emphasis is always on ideas, correcting your own, challenging others for not having them. Let me suggest another defense of your Jungian colleagues whom you say do not work the field further. Maybe they do it with feeling, in their work with people, whereas you want the advances to come through thinking ideas.*

J.H. This business of contrasting feeling and thinking doesn't do either of them any good. I am feeling now, and I am thinking— we both are. Why cut them apart? In English some of the best language for feeling, the most sensitive language is thinking language: to be "considerate," "thoughtful," "attentive." To "esteem" is another one. To be "mindful." So don't tell me those Jungians are working the field by feeling because they are not thinking. But let's be generous again: maybe the whole thing has to do with the mode of psychotherapy itself. Even the Freudians haven't produced comparable work to Freud. Their best, their most interesting writer isn't a Freudian really: Norman O. Brown, who is a classicist and never practiced a day in his life. I wonder if he ever was in analysis.

L.P. *Is it something inherent to psychotherapy, then, that inhibits theoretical advances, philosophical thinking, and working the field further? You seem to be explaining your own anger. In order to think you have to deny yourself as a Jungian practitioner, as a psychotherapist, since you are showing, with the example of Norman O. Brown, that the best thinking is done by nontherapists.*

J.H. Freud and Jung were therapists *and* thinkers, *both*. So is Laing, in his way, so is Thomas Szasz in his, and Lacan in his.

But still there is something in what we are getting at here. It's true of medicine: there are very, very few interesting ideas coming from medical practitioners. It's true probably also in theology: the interesting ideas don't come from the priests, they come from theologians or religionists like Eliade or David Miller.

L.P.   *An opposition between theory and practice?*

J. H.   Let's not make another opposition—it's just as wrong as thinking versus feeling. It may have something to do with writing, with the act of forming thoughts and feelings in words on paper. This is a practice of its own, and how many practices can you practice? Although I sometimes believe that if you write, you practice better in therapy because you're more watchful, acute, curious, or whatever.

L.P.   *But many of your Jungian colleagues write and yet you question their thinking.*

J.H.   Not *all* their thinking, not *everybody's* thinking! Goodness! What I'm getting at is that discipleship prevents thinking. In order to be loyal to Jung, they become undifferentiated. They feel their task is the mission. Spread the word. Teach. When you have to teach something, you become didactic and you have to simplify: you teach what is already finished, or let's say, when you teach something, it becomes already finished. Anyway, they are spreading the word, showing that Jung is right. I am not concerned with showing Jung is right. He *is right*—and he is wrong too . . . but that doesn't matter. There are other things to do, like follow the implications, go on, raise questions, look at what he said from underneath, in new light, strange light, bring more out of it.

L.P.   *One of the recurring themes in your critique of psychology—especially in* The Myth of Analysis *and later in* Re-Visioning Psychology—*is your attack on psychological nominalism, what you called the nominalistic denial. Your position is not new: your argument is that the language of so-called abnormal psychology is not only inadequate but also too poor. What do you mean by "too poor"?*

J.H.   By nominalism here I refer to the argument that psychiatric terms don't refer to anything real: they are fantasies, useful fictions. Or, some say, *useless* fictions. Because the terms are only conventions, only nomina, doesn't necessitate throwing them out. That's to be literal in the other direction—the antipsychiatrists are just as literal as the psychiatrists. One side holds that these labels are real and that people have or are these terms, like schizophrenic or paranoid, and the other side holds that there is no reality at all to these terms and so people aren't sick.

L.P. *How does your position differ from the antipsychiatry school identified mainly with Laing and Cooper and movements derived from them?*

J.H. If we could clear up the nominalism, give a real backing—not to the terms but to the nominalism itself—then we wouldn't have to be propsychiatry or antipsychiatry. Then we could argue about psychiatry openly from political or social positions, rather than disguising the political argument in a pseudolinguistic philosophical one. The problem is the nominalism. What are these terms: psychotic, psychosis, depressive, depression, paranoid? What kind of reality is in these words? Are they merely descriptive? Then what is the relation between the description and the person to whom the description is being applied? Suppose we gave up the idea that the terms must refer to something, suppose we accept the nominalism, completely, then we would be engaged in rhetoric and not science. Then the terms would have connotative meanings and metaphorical values. Then a patient called paranoid is acting in a certain rhetorical style—like a genre in literature or a type in the old comedy or in the Bible—and this style offers acute psychiatric observations, like: defensive, suspicious, enclosed, and isolated in special systems of thought and feeling about other people or one's own body, ideas of reference, and so on. This same pattern or something like it or aspects of it might once have been called Saturnian. Then the nominalistic terms would be backed by archetypal patterns.

L.P. *Is there no real sickness?*

J.H. That's a catch question: if I say yes, I am a realist, a psychiatrist. If I say no, I am a nominalist, a member of the antipsychiatry school. What I'm doing here doesn't deny or affirm sickness—it distinguishes the problem of language from the problem of sickness, or it imagines the foreground of sickness against the background of language, rhetoric. The "real" sickness is probably less in the style—paranoid, depressed—and more in the fixedness, the literalism with which the style is taken by the patient and the doctor. To diagnose and treat a sickness as a rhetorical style means that the doctor enter the same kind of language as the patient. I don't mean the doctor and the patient get infected by each other, some kind of *folie à deux;* I mean that they are constellated by the same archetypal pattern. Sympathy. If there is a God in the disease as Jung said, the God is already in the doctor's language when he formulates the disease into a diagnosis.

L.P. *Isn't there a danger here of simply replacing diagnostic terms with mythical terms or Gods?*

J.H. I've come out against that very often. The issue isn't finding new terms to replace the old terms. The old terms are fine. It's a matter of seeing the old terms differently, shifting away from both nominalism and realism to rhetoric and metaphor. You see, mythical language just can't be taken literally. Everybody knows these Gods don't exist and that they aren't real. We all know Venus and Saturn are images, metaphors, fantasies. But we forget that that is true of hysteria, schizophrenia, and ego, too. Mythical terms can't get literalized the same way because built into them is the sense of the fantastic—and yet, at the same time, they have the cultural value, the traditional power and universality of Gods. I recently learned at Eranos, from Professor Ueda, that concepts are all right in Zen thinking if they have in them the potential for self-correction. A good term allows seeing through itself. A good term must inherently imply that it is not literal. Myths and Gods do just that. I'm trying to shift the whole basis of psychiatric language into the field of imagination, where the disorders are anyway, where the illnesses are. That's where the language ought to be, too. I want to bring back an older and richer language into abnormal psychology. I want Venus, Aphrodite, the Goddess of sensual surfaces, of details, of intimacy to come back into the clinical descriptions. How does the patient move, dress, breathe, hold his hands; what physiognomic character is there in the face, what ethnic race, what animal, what planetary qualities, what eyes are there in front of your eyes? If you went into a threatening bar or had to size up someone in your platoon, someone your life depended on—how would you look at them and what words would you find regarding their immediate sensuous presentation? Our visual psychological language is about subjective states: how I feel; not what is in front of me. *Interesting, amazing, boring, curious, awful, amusing*—these words are about me and my feelings . . . not about you, there. They are not descriptions. I ask you, How was the train ride coming up from Italy? You can say, awful, tiring, boring—but that tells me nothing about the train ride. It tells me about your subjective state. Instead, you could say, crowded, noisy, stinky, no seats, dirty washroom, delayed, stopped in every station. Or you might give me a particular image that condenses, metaphorizes the whole trip.

L.P. *Are you sure that this kind of subjective-state language isn't American, especially? In Italian we love vivid and funny descriptive words for qualities.*

J.H. It may be especially American—at least academic America, therapeutic America. We certainly today have a cult of feeling. Most psychotherapy schools today stress introspective feeling: you are supposed to be constantly focusing and reporting on your own feelings with words like anxiety, aggression. Words without images. Actually it's completely conceptualized feeling and isn't feeling at all. Woody Allen does marvelous parodies of this. Don't you see how this ruins our appreciation of what is actually there in the world around us, its actual face? . . . If we're going to move back to things as faces, the world as alive, a presentation of Aphrodite to the nostrils and eyeballs, then we're going to have to recover the language of qualities. Is that why Flaubert told a young writer to go out and look at a tree for hours and hours? Stop writing about yourself. Get the qualities of the tree back into your language. Psychological language is the worst: aggression, hostility, dependence—what ugly empty words. They are so full and big and important that they are empty. If we trained as writers, instead of as . . . well whatever it is psychologists train as . . . we would be taught not to use such sloppy words, but to be exact and careful to present a sensuous image. Our language in psy-

chology is poverty stricken—Aphrodite driven out of it completely. These few words like "aggression" are highly charged with
emotion. Conferences on "aggression" ... psychodynamics of aggression. As if it were one of the old mediaeval vices or personifications. They aren't even words: they are ideologies. Like patriarchal or feminine or dependent.

L.P. *Could you take one of these terms apart for me. How are
they both packed or overloaded with importance and yet empty?*

J.H. Well, let's try it with depression—an old favorite. A patient
says, "I feel depressed." Now, I don't know what that means. It's
empty. No sensuous content, no image; it's loaded. The word actually is a symptom-formation, a compromise with the depression which helps repress it, only admitting it in a vague, abstract
way. So, in practice I'll want to get it precise: what do you feel?
Sad, empty, dry? Burned out? Do you feel weak, do you feel like
crying? And where do you feel depressed? In your eyes—do you
want to cry; do you cry? In your legs, are they heavy, can't get
up, can't move; in your chest, are you anxious, and how does that
feel, where, when? Is it like being tied up, or being poisoned?
What about your bowels, sexual fantasies? What color is your
mood, what is the temperature of it, the climate? You see what I
mean: we are trying to get to the Venus language: the whole
taste, body, image of the state of soul in words. All that has disappeared, and instead the big empty vapid jargon word, depression.
That's a terrible impoverishment of the actual experience.

L.P. *The impoverishment of words is always dangerous for emotions. Without adequate words, emotions become grosser. Language helps differentiate emotion—that has long been the hu-
manist viewpoint.*

J.H. Emotion seems to want this. Emotion itself invents extraordinary gestures and complicated curses and insults; just think of
the images and names coming out of sexual passion. The differ-
entiation, the nuancing of emotions, is the whole work of culture.
The modern poetry that came out of Williams and Pound and
Imagism, and Eliot, too, insisted on breaking up big emotions
into precise images. This movement came at the same time as
psychoanalysis, just before the First World War, and psychoanal-

ysis is a kind of Imagism—a way of getting the images to make emotions more precise. It's a poetic movement, psychoanalysis.

L.P. *It is quite difficult to understand your use of the term "psychoanalysis," the meaning you give to it.*

J.H. I never mean only Freud or only Freud's school. Psychoanalysis means all forms of depth psychology. And there are many forms of depth psychology. Any of these movements that takes the soul deeper or provides shadow awareness or enriches the imagination might be called psychoanalysis. When you start to do the work you seem to be preserving, you're restoring lost memory. You go back. You try to recover images from the past; you breathe, you animate the images. But that's only half of the job. And the other half of the job—if one thinks in terms of *fama* and death and what really matters—is a destruction of images, burning them out—like Kirschner, the painter, who wanted to burn his paintings, or Kafka, who wanted to destroy his writings, before they died. Forgetting. A long process of forgetting. Forgetting the petty grievances, forgetting sentimentalities. Forgetting images that are not fecund, that no longer produce. Images that the mind goes back to perhaps, but after a long process of analysis they seem to be irrelevant. Huge pieces of one's life are irrelevant. One doesn't dream of them. They're gone. You spent four years in so-and-so place when you were between eight and twelve and never once, when you're sixty years old, never once have you dreamed of that place. You had a certain school teacher for years, let's say you had a tutor all through your adolescence. Never once do you dream of the tutor. Some insignificant schoolfriend appears again and again. Some building. Some place. Some woman—and not *the* woman. The psyche makes a radical destructive selection among images and burns a lot of the paintings before death.

L.P. *Isn't this repression?*

J.H. Only if you look at it from above. I'm trying to get to another view of it. I'm trying to lift the repression from the idea of repression itself, to see it from the psyche's perspective, because we have to ask the question: who does the repressing, the forgetting? The psyche does. It just takes certain paintings out of inventory, removes them entirely, lets things go down the river, to the sea, washed away, gone.

L.P. *If you justify repression, you undermine the basis of psychoanalysis. The idea of the unconscious is built on it.*

J.H. Oh, sure . . . but just for a moment let go of the usual notion of repression that has to be lifted because an inquiring, curious, psychoanalytic mind has to feel everything, look at everything. I don't mean just getting rid of paintings you don't want to look at anymore. I'm not talking about a deliberately defensive ego. Think of it instead as something necessary to psychic economy. The psyche is very economical. Hinduism says you deal only with what belongs to your karma in this life and some things are repressed to be dealt with by another life. The psyche works according to *dharma, ananké,* necessity; it gives you only a certain pensum of work. So, as you get older the psyche begins to burn the images. But ego wants to make everything conscious. When Freud says, "Where Id was there shall Ego be"—it is also an extraordinarily greedy statement. He wants to get every last stone out of the quarry, but what about the quarry? The Greeks, the archaic people, are always giving things back. Maybe repressing and forgetting are means of sacrifice—not *my* giving it back, but the psyche making it unavailable to my greed. "There shall Ego be" is like "Let there be Light," a very big God-the-Father statement, Promethean, too, making everything available, "opening every dream," as Freud said. So we strip-mine the psyche. Our notion of making-conscious is exploitative. We burn up our psychic resources just as we burn up our natural gas, as if there were an endless supply from the so-called creative unconscious. Who said the unconscious, the depths of the psyche, is an inexhaustible creative pool? Maybe psychic burn-out results from this exploitative view—as if everything should come up and be used. No repression: open the wells. Instead, we could treasure the images. How many images does a person need? How many ideas, memories? Once the unconscious was called a *thesaurus,* a treasury, and that implies a very different attitude toward a dream. One dream could be enough for a long time if it's from the treasury. But if it's from the strip mine, the quarry, then we get into having to remember everything, overcoming the naturalness of repression. We could instead let the figures themselves decide what is to be remembered, which of them are important and want to come 'up' out of the id. Maybe they know best what is relevant to the conscious personality, rather than the conscious personality "lifting repression" from the figures. The figures of the dreams give me enough work. I don't have to dig for more, I don't have to unearth them like wrapped-up mummies—analyst as archeologist. If the figures come into my dreams, then they are asking to be talked with, received, or whatever has to happen between us.

4 THERAPY, DREAMS, AND THE IMAGINAL

L.P. *Talking about therapy; then. . . .*

J.H. It's so many different things, isn't it? . . . It's a practice of religion, a practice of magic, a practice of teaching, a practice of political brainwashing, it's a practice of change of consciousness, it's a practice of terror even; there are just an incredible variety of things happening in therapy; it's a form of love, there is coupling, there is complicity—all these things are going on in therapy. People have tried to understand why it came when it did in our historical context, other people are concerned with when is it going to be finished. I brought lots of these questions into *The Myth of Analysis*. For me therapy is basically the evocation of imagination: it's training, working, struggling with imagination. If I were to say that it has to do with healing, I'd have to say healing the imagination or healing the relationship to the imagination. If I want to say therapy has to do with raising or deepening the levels of consciousness or intensifying it, I'll still put therapy in connection with imagination as the development of a psychological sense of imagination.

L.P. *And what is a "psychological sense"?*

J.H. The fact that we ask those questions shows where we are off. Probably the hardest question I ever had to deal with is "How do you know so-and-so is psychological?" You have a trainee or you are on an examining board or you pick somebody for your doctoral program, and your colleagues say, "So-and-so is just not psychological," "So-and-so is very psychological." That is the hardest thing to define. That quality of psychological. I think that quality is like a talent in the arts. What one tries to do in therapy is make the other person, the other person's *psyche* more psychological.

L.P. *Let's try to get this more precise.*

J.H. Does psychological mean more complicated? Does it mean more profound? More sensitive? Or more metaphorical? Hearing on two levels at once: ironic, metaphorical . . . is that more psychological? Is more psychological seeing through, the ability to see through? Is it more considered and reflective, or does it mean more rooted, more instinctive sureness? Is psychological more like Jane Austen, a feeling sensitivity to nuances that are taking place between people, whether they're in their faces or in their voices or in the pressures, the atmospheric pressures in the room, is that psychological? Hard to say, isn't it?

L.P. *It is just like with films: there are films that are psychological and films that are not. Just think of a Visconti compared with a Bertolucci: they made films on the same subjects—decadence, bourgeois families, melodrama—and still there is some reason why you can say that Bertolucci's films are worse. Are they really worse? No, it's just that they lack that quality of the psychological that Visconti has.*

J.H. Therapy for me is about developing that *quality* of the psychological. I use the term "imagination" because that's part of it and I don't mean just having lots of fantasies. I mean images that resonate with depth, that don't stop the psyche from imagining further. Bertolucci closes things down in his images. They leave you in the *known* world; messages. But Visconti has an enigmatic aspect, more mythical, let's say.

L.P. *How do you make the connecting in your therapy between the personal case history of a patient and the imaginal background or the archetypal, mythical reflection?*

J.H. It's a way of hearing and reacting. You don't make connections; they are already there. Hermes makes the connections, and if you push too hard to make one, you elbow out Hermes. "The hidden connection is the best," Heraclitus said. What could it mean? It could mean not seeing the connection but hearing it, smelling it, fingering it. You have to listen for what's going on with an ear that is *not* attuned to the same wave length as the patient's story. There's a jarring, a discomfort. It's not supportive understanding and sympathetic being-in-tune. It's more a curious hearing things differently.

L.P. *It sounds again very literary, like Pinter?*

J.H. Or even the most realist dramatists. Ibsen and Chekhov, say. People just talk usual sentences and you hear the imaginal background: it's all much more profound, tragic, comic, than what seems to be only personal social realism.

L.P. *Is there then no move toward showing which archetypes are at work? Don't you point out the senex or the puer or the child or Persephone or Hera in a person's behavior or story?*

J.H. I listen for the rhetoric and watch the behavior, sure. But using a myth or a mythical figure as a label doesn't help at all. Therapy isn't a demonstration of the Gods. It has to be epiphanic: they have to come forth and surprise us. Of course, it helps to know a little beforehand about their styles—how they tend to appear.

L.P. *About rhetoric. You use "rhetoric" in a peculiar way, you speak of myths appearing in rhetoric, in speech styles; each of these styles appropriate to what is really going on in the psyche. And you say you are not looking for a specific mythic definition: but a myth is always something that is defined, and in a way it is a fixed pattern. . . .*

J.H. Yes, yes. It has a pattern to it. I assume several things: I assume that whatever goes on is purposeful; that is a rule, you know. I assume that whatever goes on is intelligible, not understandable, intelligible. There's a difference. Understanding requires a hermeneutic: you bring a set of concepts to bear on what is in front of you, while "intelligible" as I think of it means simply presentable, things as they present themselves. They are phenomena: that is, they bear a light in them, they shine, they can be seen. And when we understand them, we darken that light, because we make suppositions about them, instead of letting them speak as they are to the imagination. This is very important, but awfully hard to talk about, because I haven't found my way through it yet.

There's a huge set of ideas I'm trying to work on right now

that has to do with this addiction to understanding, to hermeneutics. I am trying to work out how hermeneutics interferes with presentation, or let's say, how hermeneutics creates an intelligibility at the expense of the presented intelligibility of phenomena and we become deluded by our understanding. I guess I am trying to become a naive realist, as they say in philosophy, or a phenomenalist—but with a twist, because I want to talk about events as they appear to the *imagination*, as images. Maybe dreams can help us here; maybe I can show you what I mean by dreams. When I'm dreaming at night, I'm in the image, I'm imagining—or imagining is going on and I am sunk deep into the inherently intelligible, the sense-making, clear, amazingly purposeful life of the dream. And almost the moment I wake up, even if very slowly wake up, my understanding begins. I'm understanding, turning the dream into understanding it, even if I don't want to, and at that moment the dream fades. It gets obscure, too, and loses its intelligibility. Why is that, why? The dream is hiding from my understanding. It's almost like an inner poet who hides from the inner critic, because he doesn't want to be understood and found out what he *means*.

L.P. *Imagination resists hermeneutics. Is this a new theory of resistance? Or, is this the old romantic notion of the imagination and of two worlds, nightworld and dayworld?*

J.H. I don't know. It could be the archaic idea of two souls and that the dream soul once it gets a life of its own—and I've been dreaming and thinking of my dreams constantly for more than thirty years—doesn't like mixing in with the day soul that also has been getting stronger or brighter. You see, I don't think this is only my own problem or only the problem of older people who dream less, supposedly. I think it has to do with hermeneutics. If we go at a phenomenon in order to understand that phenomenon, no matter what system of hermeneutics you use, something happens about making it unintelligible in order to save it. If we regard all events as already intelligible, that they're already speaking in an inherently intelligible way; one watches, responds, dances, whatever it is, with the event, which is different from the understanding of the event.

L.P. *So what is your attitude when you are presented with a dream in therapy?*

J.H. It's so different. Sometimes I laugh like crazy. Dreams are so amazing—the things they think up. The details they bother to put in. A lot of the time I feel sunk, almost ill. It's too much—I mean the hermeneutic task is too much. I just don't see a thing here, don't feel anything, except my own being knocked back and helpless, and it will take maybe forty minutes of patient, careful, persistent work, and I mean *work*, to bring that dream to life, to break it open, to get in touch with it. Then sometimes I move in so fast that I get insensitive to the dreamer, as if he or she didn't matter at all, but that the dream catches me on fire, and I am burning to talk about it or, better, talk to it. I talk more *to the dream* than to the patient.

You see this comes from a view of what a human being is. These images make one realize that the patient, me, you, is only relatively real. The images are what really count, and they get so little place in our world, so my job is to let them speak and to speak with them. This is an idea of Jung's who said, "In a certain way these figures are as real as we are real." Or Corbin, who said, "It is not your individuation, it's the angel's individuation that is one's task." Then one can't help but be discreet, because you are not fully the author of your own dreams and the authority comes from them, you speak in a sense for the images. If you take psychic reality as really real—not just as a bunch of complexes or the effect of society or the result of earlier development—but just as real as the bricks and the stones and the trees, then you are limited by that reality. And you become careful, discreet.

L.P. *A Freudian would say that giving such a reality to the images is a way of getting rid of the reality principle. Even more: by emphasizing the image instead of the person, you make the therapist, yourself, an unreal image.*

J.H. That's just what I mean about being discreet. You as a person have to step back so that the images can come forward. The theory of transference has overvalued the analyst, and in all therapy one knows that one is a "projected image." It isn't only that one is a projected image; it is that the analyst has absorbed the imagination of the patient, even replaced it, so his views, his thoughts, her views, her thoughts tend to dominate what goes on. So the analyst has to get out of the way. That's the whole problem all the time in everything, standing in the way of images, and that's true no matter what you do. Even in this interview we have to get out of the way of it, so it can happen by itself, with just a little help here and there from us.

It's just like analysis: let *it* come up, without so much personalizing of the analyst or of the patient. They are the means by which analysis goes on and that's what people are in the room for, for the analysis, not for themselves; just like our conversation now, it's for the sake of the interview not for us. If it were just us, we wouldn't know what to say, to talk about. We don't have anything really to talk about: you don't know me, I don't know you, yet look at the interview—it's moving right along. The interview seems to know what it wants from us. You see, the analyst is in the same sort of place. He, the analyst, doesn't really know that much, doesn't know which way this person's fate is going to go, doesn't know why these symptoms are occurring fundamentally: of course, he always has clues about it, but he doesn't know as much as the psyche knows.

L.P.   *This is rather a radical statement to make!*

J.H.   The psyche is *not* unconscious. *We* are, we patients, we analysts. The psyche is constantly making intelligible statements. It's making dreams and symptoms, it's making fantasies and moods. It's extraordinarily intentional, purposive. But the system of therapy has projected "the unconscious" into the patient's psyche, which, then because of opposites, means that the analyst must be conscious. Both patient and analyst tend to believe this system. But the point is that consciousness floats; a psychic fluidum, as Mesmer might have called it, wrapping around and all through the analytical session. It doesn't belong to either party. Sometimes the patient has an insight, and another moment the analyst is conscious by simply being reticent, and another moment the consciousness is really in the image.

For instance, a black snake comes in a dream, a great big black snake, and you can spend a whole hour with this black snake talking about the devouring mother, talking about the anxiety, talking about the repressed sexuality, talking about the natural mind, all those interpretive moves that people make, and what is left, what is vitally important, is what that snake is doing, this crawling huge black snake that's walking into your life . . . and the moment you've defined the snake, interpreted it, you've lost the snake, you've stopped it, and then the person leaves the hour with a concept about my repressed sexuality or my cold black passions or my mother or whatever it is, and you've lost the snake. The tasks of analysis is to keep the snake there, the black snake, and there are various ways for keeping the black snake . . . see, the black snake's no longer necessary the moment it's been interpreted, and you don't need your dreams any more because they've been interpreted.

But I think you need them all the time, you need that very image you had during the night. For example, a policeman, chasing you down the street . . . you need that image, because that image keeps you in an imaginative possibility . . . if you say, "Oh, my guilt complex is loose again and is chasing me down the street," it's a different feeling, because you've taken up the unknown policeman into your ego system of what you know, your guilt. You've absorbed the unknown into the known (made the unconscious conscious) and nothing, absolutely nothing has happened, nothing. You're really safe from that policeman, and you can go to sleep again. Your interpretation protects your sleep. I want to let the psyche threaten the hell out of you by keeping that policeman there chasing you down the street, even now as we talk. The policeman is more important than what we say about him: I mean *the image is always more inclusive, more complex* (it's a complex, isn't it?) *than the concept*. Let's make that a rule. That's why "stick to the image" is another rule in archetypal psychology. So who is the policeman? Is he guilt, or is he the sense of the law, is he the sense of order, is he the sense of the city, the *polis?* Has he something to do with an inherent structure of consciousness that wants something from you, or reminds you of something, calls you to him? Otherwise he wouldn't be chasing you. You need to keep the policeman there so that you can learn what he is up to and what keeps you running, and running in the street, into the street.

The images are where the psyche is. People say, "I don't know what the soul is," or "I've lost my soul" or whatever. To me the place to look when you feel that way is immediately to the images that show where you are with your soul in your dreams. "I don't know where the hell I am, I am all confused, I've just lost my job . . . everything is happening." Where do you look when you feel that way? . . . The place to look is not only to your feelings, not to your interpretations, not ask help from a third person necessarily, but ask yourself what were you in the image? Where's your imagination? That immediately *locates* you somewhere, into your own psyche. Whereas the introspection doesn't help at all, chasing one's shadow, questioning why did I do this, why do I do that and why did they do this. An instant turmoil: the Hindus call it *vritta,* turning the mind on itself like an anthill. But when you have an image of an anthill you know where you are: you're in the middle of an anthill, they're going in fifty different directions at once, *but the ants are <u>doing</u> something.* It seems desperate to me only because I say it shouldn't be an anthill. But an anthill has an internal structure, it is an organization. So the gift of an image is that it affords a place to watch your soul, precisely what it is doing.

L.P.   *But is it then possible to have a different view of the image? Not an interpretation?*

J.H.   Of course, if instead of the language of concept—the anthill is your confusion (and then you think, "Oh, I always get confused; when somebody leaves me, I get confused; when I get rejected, I don't know where I am; I just walk in a thousand different directions"—and you begin with subjectivism, that subjective importance about yourself). Instead of that kind of language, you can talk to the confusion in the language of the image, which is an anthill. The ants are swarming: some are going up, some are coming down, some are carrying eggs somewhere, some are taking care of I don't know what, carrying a dead one. . . . there's a great deal going on, let's see what the ants are doing. And I am not thinking about confusion anymore, I'm *watching the phenomenon,* and seeing phenomenologically what is happening. I am no longer caught in my own subjectivity. I'm fascinated with what's going on, and this attentiveness is quieting. I can see it scientifically—watch as a naturalist does. The phenomenologist of the psyche is also a naturalist of the psyche, watching the way it produces what it produces. I might see the ants suddenly all eating each other up. It's no use saying that is a destructive scene that's happening: I have to wonder about purposefulness, too. Let's watch: maybe the psyche is taking care of the problem by itself. We don't know in advance; we have to stick with the image, stay in the imagination. "Oh, oh, they just started crawling on my feet, eating my feet. I can't stand it. They are crawling up my legs. I'm going crazy." Now the image is vividly coming to life. Still, stay with it, what is your reaction? I can brush them off, I can run around in circles. I can get a dish of honey to attract them elsewhere. I can sing them an ant-song. You see, I can do something in relationship to the actual thing that is happening. But what I don't do, won't do is interpret the ants. You saw that move—"They're crawling up my legs. I'm going crazy"—that shift from image to interpretation—and *that* makes you crazy.

The hermeneutic move made the craziness. Who says you are going crazy? What you actually feel is the ants crawling up your legs. Then there are other questions to be put into this scene. I mean you have to locate yourself in it, extend the terrain a bit, not a lot, not too much, but a bit. Have you stepped on the ants, have you tried to cross their path, have you put your foot unknowingly into an anthill? Step away! It's a certain animal movement. An animal sense of living. This is the active relation to the image that we want to get going through therapy.

L.P. *But the verbal language seems to have little importance in your view, almost a negative role. Verbal language has always been one of the root-metaphors in psychoanalysis. It was for Freud, who equated the system of images in dreams to the system of a language and put on the same level the use of verbal language and the like images within the dream. And Jung used verbal language a great deal and never questioned it: the whole idea of psychoanalytical therapy is the idea of a talking cure—two people in a room, talking.*

J.H. Sure, I think in concepts . . . we're modern civilized people, we need our concepts. Of course, I don't mean throw out all conceptual language, but, generally speaking, conceptual language is where we're caught, where we are in the ego, where things are dead, where we go back to what is already made and finished and where the images can't reach us. So another way of talking to an image is to play with the language around the image, about ants, about bugs, about going bugs, to begin to play with words, so that you are breaking reforming them and getting the metaphor out of them or cutting them into a pun ... very important, the verbal mode of working with the image, the poetic mode of working with the image, releases their meanings that were concealed in the phonemes, concealed in the etymology. The word in the dream is not restricted to conceptual interpretation because the word in the dream is not a concept. It's an image arriving out of imagination, and the dictionary meaning, the denotation of the word, is only part. But this is well known.

It is already in Freud in the *Traumdeutung*. Though he only has part of it. Other Freudians since then have gone on with that. Jungians haven't: they are not sophisticated with language, for better or for worse. I mean that they may be sophisticated about symbolic thinking but their use of language is literal, unreflected, so that they get caught in the trap they think they have escaped from. There is a great deal more to do with the fixed meanings of the words in dreams, and with all our language. Again, hermeneutics isn't up to the multilayered, the polytheistic speech of the dream. Hermeneutics is monotheistic. I guess what Lacan and those Yalies, those Frenchies, have been trying to do with their destructuralizing is getting hermeneutics off of its monotheistic basis and into a kind of talking back to the image that is as "crazy," as polytheistic, as the image itself.

Anyway, there are lots of simple things you can do to break up the literal sense of your dream interpretations, those fixed meanings inherent in our usual language. That literalism, that dayworld rational secular commonsense has to be overcome again and again when you do psychological work. For instance: most people in analysis write their dreams and tell their dreams in sentences. If you take the punctuation out of the dream, so that you're looking at it the way you would look at an ancient Babylonian or Hebrew text, where you don't know quite whether that's an *ayn* or whether that's an *alef*, you don't know what it is, you

don't know really what to do, and then you get about ten different possibilities about that text. Freud used the same metaphor
for the dream: an ancient text.

L.P. *But Freud had a whole theory about the content of the
dream and the different layers of meaning of a dream. And the
same with Jung, although in a different way.*

J.H. We're talking about *animating the images*, not content of
dreams. This is the crucial job now. It's not a question of symbolic
contents, not a question of recognizing that there are images or
that images are important. We have, since Freud, since 1900, this
great *Traumdeutung*, where he said, "My goodness, look at the
dreams!" The dreams—all these images in your dreams are significant, tremendously significant. And then Jung said, "All those
images going on in psychotics are tremendously significant. The
fantasies, the dreams, the images are going on forever in the collective unconsciousness. They're the background of art, they're
the background of madness, they're the background of thought,
the background of childhood thinking, the background of ritual . . .
it's everywhere. The images, the imagination, is fundamental."

But then what they actually did was to make a move that we
no longer want to do. Their move, that they both made, was to
translate the images into crystallized symbolic meanings. That is,
they took whatever they saw and didn't leave it where it was, but
moved it into "this *means* that." I don't want to go into the details of their systems of translation. Put it another way—they
brought up the material and then by the translation sent it back
down again. Once you've translated the dream into your Oedipal
situation or your omnipotence fantasy or your penis-envy or
you've translated the big black snake into the mother, the Great
Mother, you no longer need the image, and you let the image
only say one thing, one word: Great Mother. Then it disappears.
You don't want that black snake really any more. You want to
work on your mother complex, change your personality and so
on. Now this still leaves the soul unanimated. That is, unalive.
The images are not walking around on their own legs. They've
been turned into meanings. As somebody said about Jung, his
whole myth was the myth of meaning. Now let's leave meaning,
and the search for meaning, and the meaning of life.

L.P. *So, it's not the meaning of life as with Jung or the interpretation of life as with Freud, let us say, but the imagination of life.*

J.H. Yes, that's good. Why I have so much antagonism to therapy is that in many ways it's so antiimaginative. Dreams are extraordinary, people's lives are extraordinary, unbelievable; fantastic things happening all the time . . . they walk into therapy with these images, these absurdities, this surrealism, and it's translated into the deadest, dullest, most serious, most unimaginative . . . a bore, an utter bore. Jesus! Hermeneutics is like an academic cafeteria line, in-jokes and bad food, and self-serving (there's a joke, right there). No. Instead of hermeneutics we have to let in the puer aspect of what goes on in one's life . . .

L.P. *. . . then the imagination of life requires a puer approach, and your mode of therapy is a puer mode? By puer I mean what you have sketched out in your book* Puer Papers—*the youthful spirit archetype, the eternally youthful, fresh and originating. This approach would mean a therapy that is winged and inspired and fantastic and irresponsible and probably also unrelated . . .*

J.H. Hold on here. That was the puer speaking just now, attacking most analysis as unimaginative, as senex and making that joke. Of course, that's not the whole of it. Analysis doesn't belong to any single God. But I don't mind saying that for me to do therapy requires a close feeling of the puer, a kind of infusion of the puer archetype. I'm very familiar with that style and its shadows.

L.P. *What are they?*

J.H. Inflation, mainly. Inflating myself and the patient and seeing mainly positive things and encouraging things to fly and take fire, evoking the aerial anima and forgetting the earth, and keeping free of close entanglements like transference, by-passing the parents for the ancestors, the culture. . . .

L.P. *That could be helpful for some kinds of conditions, but how does this puer approach with its shadows work with a person who is strongly a puer type?*

J.H. Hmm . . . *folie à deux.* Both of us burning our wings together. But mainly that's not what happens. What happens is rather an analytical irony that lets me see through the puer games. And don't forget that where there is a puer, there is senex and anima, and the pattern gets complicated, and things don't just fly and burn. There is sadness and sensitivity. Oh, lots of anguish—so soon one is mortal again. The archetypes seem to self-correct, if allowed their extension.

L.P. *It sounds as if you only work with young men in therapy, but I know that these "wings" are very relevant for the analysis of women. Women, too, can be caught between the old father of tradition and the young revolutionary spirit.*

J.H. Like the many young women leading the different revolutions. But in therapy, the puer attitude isn't just revolution. It shows a way out of the fears and traps and the fixed ideas—those principled opinions that take hold of some women's consciousness, what's called "animus." The puer's interested in spirit—anybody's spirit, so it doesn't fix women into being Great Yin Carriers, a whole earth catalog. So what I mean by the puer attitude in therapy isn't at all restricted to young men, and it certainly isn't some sort of method. Therapy has everything possible going on in it, and it needs every sort of tool. Look at the instruments dentists have, drawers of little tools and nozzles, and that's just for your teeth. Imagine what's needed for the psyche!

L.P. *You said that phenomena of the unconscious like dreams and images, generally speaking, are purposeful, and intelligible, and spontaneous. This is Jung's concept, the idea of* telos, *a final aim or purpose. Every psychic event in neurosis or psychosis has a* telos, *in other words, it is a creation.*

J.H. Jung's notion of *telos* is crucial. Most theories of psychology regard what happens as socially caused, parentally caused, biologically caused. But if you assume that an event is autogenerative, as Jung did, then you say, "This is a psychological creation, and it has to be understood in its own terms." This means we have to use aesthetic criteria for psychological events because they are creative products. Now, that raises a lot of different kinds of questions about psychotherapy. So the analysis of the parents and the analysis of the social conditions and the analysis of the education and the analysis of the history, all are there, because they go into anything that happens—an event has those things in it; the raspberry here on the table in front of you has historical, biological, economic conditions in it. Conditioning is right there in the psyche simultaneous with the creative, with the spontaneous. You shouldn't separate the creative from the conditioned because the new is always tied with the old. The mistake is only when you see only the new or only the old, when you reduce the new to the old or neglect the old in the new.

L.P. *Are you implying here a notion of creativity inherent to all psychic events? Is there a positive aspect to everything the psyche produces?*

J.H. Let's be careful here. The fact that a psychic event is a creative event doesn't mean "creative, isn't that beautiful!" or "creative is romantic" and all that crap; no, not only positive, because creative also means destructive; and this comes from Jung, too, who says, "Creative means both destructive and constructive," so it doesn't have a positive happy evaluation only, that word "creative."

L.P. *Freud said a dream is a little psychosis, so a dream is an autonomous product of the psyche with a purpose, intelligible, and it's a creation. It means that it is a whole little creation, necessary and not superficial, not trivial. It is created necessarily in that soul and for that soul.*

J.H. That has an even further implication. If each dream is creative then each person is creative. I mean creativity doesn't mean that everybody can paint and write like a genius, but that creativity is a basic human instinct, like eating and fighting, like Jung said.

L.P. *You wrote about that in* The Myth of Analysis: *"Why can't the common man change his heroically romantic nineteenth-century concept of genius, so charged with ambition and envy, and be done with this fantasy of the extraordinary personality? Even without artistic talent, even without good fortune, at least one form of the creative is continuously open for each of us: psychological creation. And psychological creation is just the task of generating psychological reality in one's life, reanimating life."*

J.H. Psychological creation can go on anywhere, like this between us. Between people, in conversations, in families . . . even in the craziest emotions if we stand them, if we work with them, if we imagine ourselves engaged as artists in life, if we use artists as our models instead of sober teachers and sterile doctors and administrators, then we would work with the daily mess in our lives as the material for psychological creativity. And that is what therapy, as I try to do it, is all about: to get people to live their lives more from an artist fantasy of themselves, in touch with their daimon, their genius—to live like their dreams, a little psychosis, as you said—which doesn't mean at all that they have to be artists, or be geniuses, or "be creative." They don't have to prove it by producing something. I want to get far, far away from creative in the romantic sense. I mean having gratitude toward what one is given, for out of that one makes one's life, or to say it differently: you don't have to become creative because the psyche is already that; right in its mess there is creation going on. The artist fantasy of oneself accepts the mess, likes it, needs it. It's the administrator and the cleaning-lady fantasy of oneself that can't put up with one's mess. We don't have to be artists but we can change the model, the fantasy we live by, so that we don't have to imagine ourselves dull and sober and rational and critical, changing it to one that invites the puer in, and all his dangers, too. And I don't mean that everyone must become a puer or is a puer—I mean to let in the puer, that's all, and that's sometimes enough.

L.P. *At the same time that you invite the puer, you focus so much on shadow conditions like weakness, failure, depression. So it seems you perform therapy mainly within the archetype of the puer-senex.*

J.H. Yes, the senex all the time, too. But not the senex professional thing. I am very uncomfortable with the official, institutional aspects of practice. People need to see from the beginning that the therapist is an ordinary person, just another human being. If therapy is to reanimate ordinary life then it has to happen in a daily mundane setting and we have to be just as we are.

L.P. *But why do you keep the senex pattern of one hour, then?*

J.H. One hour has to do with death, and the ritual of it: you have to have that hour, you have to have the framework, a box, a situation which constellates death:—this hour will be over within five minutes—and you have to have ritual because the psyche moves through ritual. I can be downstairs chatting, my wife's seeing a patient, I'm seeing a patient, those two patients happen to know each other, so and so and so, we're all standing and we are just before our hours: we go up the stairs, my wife takes her person into her room, I take my person into my room, and the conversation is completely different: one enters the room, you've moved through the doorway, we're in another place, you enter the sanctuary, or you've walked through the propylaeum, something has happened. The conversation changes. The place is different. I'm not exaggerating it, but it's different; a *temenos* is established. You must have that framework . . . I think you can't just do analysis sitting on a park bench: I used to think you could and now I'm not so sure. You can have a good psychological conversation on a park bench, but the sanctuary of the *tomb* is constellated by the analytical room. Of course, psyche can happen in a cafe, it can happen anywhere. But the ritual process of analysis is a process through time, the cooking of the soul through time, it has to have its own form, and the practitioner's closet can help produce this form.

L.P.   *It is strange listening to you about therapy, strange that you can use both cafe and tomb as "placings" for it. This kind of strange juxtaposition comes out in your book,* The Dream and the Underworld, *which is very dark and at the same time very free, very humorous. Perhaps you should be read in the genre of black comedy.*

J.H.   The way I have written about psychoanalysis and the way I practice it do relate events to death. Not to success, not to cures. Those things happen: people do get better jobs, people do get married, and I'm delighted if they do, delighted if they don't. Delighted if whatever happens in life works out better for them. But that isn't the point of psychoanalysis. Soul is the point. It's not to further, to lubricate adaptation, to make it slide along better. It's more a matter of evoking the sense of individuality which comes with death, with fate. My death. It's very hard to stay with that. And what does death do to each moment in my life. This interview itself has to be connected to death; what's the point of sitting here talking, unless something is said that matters. The cafe *and* the tomb. The tomb must touch our talking enough to make it worth while. It isn't just to have a successful interview so that many copies of the book are read or so that ideas are explained simply and everybody can understand or to do an interview that pleases us and we have fun doing it. It's not that. The life aspect is not enough.

Something has to be touched that sets one back for a minute—that rocks you back and you say, "My God! Something is happening here. . . ." Whether we are able to do that or not, who knows—but that moment of importance comes about through connecting what we do and say with death.

L.P. *And yet it isn't tragic. You do not have a tragic style or a tragic view of therapy.*

J.H. It isn't tragic, but it gives seriousness. What we need is a ground of seriousness which does not require the tragic. The tragic seems to develop a huge ego. The tragic applies to the biggest figures. It swells one with inflation. To feel one's tragedy makes you feel terribly, terribly important. We have to get to a seriousness that does not involve the 'problem of good and evil'—tragedy tends to have that Manichaean problem in it. Now, tragedy offers three things—a, seriousness; b, importance, significance; and c, necessity. Necessity as "it couldn't be otherwise, it had to be this way." Can't we keep the necessity, the Greek *ananké,* without the heroic tragic inflation? For the Greeks, *ananké* was involved in everything, but not everything was tragic. So, we can take therapy very seriously and what goes on as very important and as necessity, but that doesn't mean it has to be tragic—that leaves it open for comic possibilities. What's strange about fate is that it has so many comic twists, even happy endings. There is a cafe, too, you know, and it provides chairs for freaks and crazies and depressives, too. After all, our fate, as Jung said, appears in our images—and they aren't all tragic, even if they require seriousness from us.

L.P. *The therapeutic relationship with the analyst, then, plays less of a role in your therapy than the therapeutic relationship with the world of images, the imaginal or the imagination.*

J.H. Look out: don't make too sharp a difference between the relationship to the analyst and the relationship to the world of images. After all, the analyst—and the patient, too—are images in the world of images, are enacting fantasies. I just prefer to start with the fantasy rather than with the person, that's all. And fantasies are not so light, not so easy.

L.P. *Let me put in here what you wrote about that in* The Myth of Analysis. *"Let us not believe that fantasy is an easy business. When Freud's patients lay down and began to reminisce, they found their fantasies embarrassing. . . . Freud also found them embarrassing . . . teller and listener did not look at each other. The shame about our fantasies gives testimony to their importance. . . . I do indeed resist telling my daydreams, my scorching hatreds, my longings and fears and their uncontrollable imagery. My fantasies are like wounds; they reveal my pathology. . . . Fantasies are incompatible with my usual ego. . . . We are not embarrassed in the same way by our will and intelligence; indeed, we proudly exhibit their accomplishments. But what breeds in the imagination is an inner world . . . the inner aspect of consciousness. These affections and fantasies are the imaginal or unconscious aspect of everything we think and do. This part of the soul that we keep to ourselves is central to analysis, to confession, to prayer, central between lovers and friends, central in the work of art, central to what we mean by 'telling the truth' and central to our fate."*

J.H. Yes, fantasies are very precious. They need supportive therapy. Therapy is a kind of mothering—not of the ego—a mothering of the images which anyway mother us, coming to us every night, helping us have a good night's sleep.

L.P. *So active imagination is central to your therapy.*

J.H. Why this active imagination is so central in therapy is because basically I don't know what way to go with the patient. It isn't that I don't have years of doing it or that it's a lack of skill or lack of training or stupidity. Certainly I have my share of stupidity—but what I mean is there is a fundamental lack of knowing what the psyche wants. Psyche knows more what it wants with itself than I may be able to imagine or interpret. I want to follow its intelligence. So if a particular image begins to appear—let's say the door opens in a dream or in a fantasy and a little girl walks in with a bunch of tulips. Marybelle walks in, in a little blue dress. Here is a spontaneous appearance. An apparition, an epiphany or, just simply, a fantasy. And for me to say, "Oh, that's your childishness or your infantility or your anima that hasn't grown up yet. . . ." Imagine someone saying to Dante that Beatrice was his anima that hadn't grown up yet, that he still was infantile. Or, saying that to Petrarch about Laura. See. But we do say those things today. And if Petrarch, if Dante walked into analysis, there would be something immediately wrong with his having fallen in love with a girl child in a red dress in church. That would have been some sort of complex.

So Mary Bell comes in with her tulips. One has to see our reactions to her as part of the history of psychoanalysis. This history of psychoanalysis will reduce her to something wrong, because that's the job of psychoanalysis, to find something wrong and cure it. Now I don't want to get rid of Maribel under any conditions. She is exactly what she is—a phenomenon. The work is to save the phenomena. So she is a phenomenon, she walks in with a bunch of tulips, and we begin to work imaginatively with this. What does she do? What does she say? If she said nothing and does nothing, one can begin to play with the image—not just associations, like tulips come in the spring, tulips are a Northern flower, tulips come from Holland. Associations of a personal level which again reduce the image of the tulips. If you looked at a Vermeer painting and you see tulips in a bowl, or a Dutch painting of the eighteenth century, a seventeenth-century still-life, you wouldn't start talking about tulips coming from Holland and tulips meaning this and this. You'd look at the image, study it, feel it, enjoy it; or you let the image express itself in its own language. We can even play with the language of tulips: Tu-lips; two-lips; Tu-lips, and Marie Belle, Bella, the sound of the words, the bell and Mary. Mirabelle. Mirabile. We can play all kinds of imaginative games, imaginative explorations of the image, the visual image, and the language of the image—and the emotion of the image, too. Because one is embarrassed by having this little girl come in: I don't know what to do with her; I wish she weren't there because she just makes me feel annoyed; and she won't talk when I want her to talk and tell me why she's there. She just hangs around and hangs on me and makes me feel burdened. Or there'll be another kind of emotion—a kind of sudden break-down into sensitivity, tenderness: Oh, my goodness, this is what's come! So there'll be an emotion that goes with it, too. And eventually what one wants is to let that image speak more and more. Either you react through these imaginative-emotional modes that I'm talking about or the voice of Marybelle begins itself to speak and say something and says why it has come. What it wants.

I can think of endless examples of this: a man is reading, he's an old man, sixty years old, he has no wife, he has no family, he never married; and while he's reading a psychological text, a voice breaks into his room and says "Where have you been, Fa-ther?" This is a tremendous startling event. "Where have you been, Father?" No one had called him father before. He has no children. He tried to answer this voice with a whole series of psychological interpretations: Oh, this voice must be the inner anima; this voice must be the young boy whom I dreamed of three nights ago. . . . He began a whole lot of psychological expla-nations which never responded directly to the voice. He never seriously thought: "Where *have* I been? What does this child want? It evidently has felt neglected; it's some child whom I've never talked to; it's my own child! And so on. He didn't get into a real conversation with the voice. Then he tried to get the child to come back and it didn't come back. The voice didn't come back. Training the person to whom the fiction or the figure or the dream or the epiphany comes to respond adequately, genuinely is three-quarters of the work.

L.P. *Don't you think that your kind of therapy can be called shamanistic? You bring other people to see daimons, visions. This can be considered quite dangerous by many people.*

J.H. This business of danger. Ugh! Goddammit! This idea of dan-ger begins in the analyst's mind. Before we get into what *people* think, *analysts* have their own set of dangers that they're imagin-ing. *They* worry, they have *their* fears. And they're afraid that the patient will commit suicide: number one fear. Or, second fear, that the patient will seduce them or they will seduce the patient. Sexual involvement. Third, violence. Fear of violence. The patient will be violent or be violent in the hour or shoot the analyst. These are all what we might call fears of regression. Oh, yes, and fear of psychosis, of course. (And fear of not paying the bill, too, let's not forget.) So—anything that seems to be spontaneous, like Marie Belle's appearance with tulips, evokes the fears, all these deeper fears of the spontaneous or the eruptive. The *invenio:* the coming-in of something. Now this coming-in—*invenio*—is also an invention in English. That is, it's a creation of the psyche. When the psyche invents something like Marybelle, it is an incursion, a coming-in. And if we can't accept these things that come in, then we're cutting out or blocking out the creative, inventive aspect of the psyche. I don't like the word "creative" there. Inventive aspect. Much simpler.

L.P. *But still, there is a kind of invasion on the part of images, and there is an attempt to raise or to evoke what's not there.*

J.H. But she *is* there. She came in on her own.

L.P. *She is independent, like a ghost or a trance figure . . .*

J.H. . . . like the start of a poem, too. Why put it right away into spiritualist, into parapsychological language: trance, ghost? Poetry starts, too, with a presence, the coming-in of an image. Robert Duncan can tell you about this quite clearly.

L.P. *Patients aren't poets.*

J.H. But maybe there is a poetic basis to their disorder; I mean, maybe blocking out their imaginative presences gives them their trouble. And, you know what blocks out the figures, the images? The strong ego.

L.P. *The usual rule in therapy is that active imagination should not be used as a technique until there is first a strong ego that can handle these comings-in of independent, autonomous complexes.*

J.H. Maribel is not a technique—and yes, she is a complex as a complexity, a complication—but she isn't mine. The strong ego is also an imaginal figure. It's the one that doesn't lose control, doesn't give over to what comes in. It's the suppressive master of the psyche: an idealized figure that we are supposed to identify with and lose consciousness of. Psychologists have been for years developing these strong egos, and of course the figures can only come in through cracks, breakdowns, broken windows, in other words, through symptoms. As long as you're going to create a castle, the psyche can only come in as an invader. And instead of it being an invention it becomes an invasion. And then you have the fears of being overwhelmed, carried away, raped. . . . So if we abandon the fantasy of Colonel Strong Ego and simply welcome what comes as a good host, as someone in the Middle Ages would have done: Maribel in a blue dress with tulips, my goodness! This is an angel?! This is a demon?! One immediately engages with it and wants to know where it came from, what it's come for, what its message is. Who are you, lovely child? Why did you come into my life? You wouldn't start off in the Middle Ages or in another culture by thinking, this means psychosis. You would start off by engaging the image. Simply, naively, phenomenally. Not with an interpretive system based on fear which is the historical ego who must exclude the image.

Now there are various reactions that we do. Sometimes we attack the image by interpretation or allegory: these are forms of exorcising it. They get rid of the image or make use of the image for one's own purposes. We ask it for help, for information, we want it to be a guide. But if you read a Greek play, they don't talk to the Gods that appear in that modern way. And anyone who has any connections with visions or mystical literature or simply the way people lived for a thousand years in Europe knows that you don't exorcise something *until you know what it is*. The discrimination of these figures is a very important thing. But you can't discriminate from a set of principles, you have to discriminate psychologically. Because it's hairy or shaggy or red or has a tail doesn't mean it's necessarily a bad thing: the symbol systems do help one discriminate, but you have to let it show its own face to begin with. The first face may be a mask; the second, too. These images change. And also the image works as a container: a container for thoughts, events, reflections, memory.

In the Renaissance and in the Middle Ages and back in classical tradition people developed an *arte della memoria,* a whole set of practices for the use of the images as containers for memory and thought. Giulio Camillo's *Teatro della Memoria* was organized like a theater where the images of the Gods grouped into sections and made order of all your thoughts, events, and rhetorical modes. They were carriers, containers, of the psyche. Ficino, Bruno, Campanella met the figures through a kind of active dramatic dialogue, that is, a kind of active imagination. Vico had four great *illustri*—eminent men whom he regarded as his tutors: he talked to them, not just dedicated his books to them or thought about them. And we walk around nowadays surrounded by images that are already in our lives: through cinema, through television, through songs; they are always there, and don't tell me that those images are not modifying our lives, affecting our psychological environment, behaving like ghosts walking into our flats!

L.P. *So therapy would be going on also during a TV serial, or at the movies. . . .*

J.H. Of course! Therapy can take place in more places than in an analytical room between two people: then you talk about therapy in the old ritual style.

L.P. *That's how you were just talking about it: the closed room necessary to constellate death.*

J.H. Necessary to constellate death. But let's not get too consistent, let's not get too monotheistic. I mean therapy of another sort goes on in a lecture, in a room with a large group of people. Psychotherapy is a service of the soul, taking care of it, and that care can happen anywhere. Watching TV can move an image, bring a realization, affect the soul, and set up a therapeutic situation inside yourself. We're all in therapy all of the time really. There's always one part of oneself which is a patient and another part trying to work on that part. It doesn't happen only when you go to a professional—though then it ought to happen best, because, as I said, death is there.

L.P. *Where else then does therapy of soul go on especially well?*

J.H. Oh, it has been really strongly going on in the feminist movements, some of the ecology movements, and some of the left-wing movements of the sixties, and today the "urban movement." It's amazing the psychological acuity and depth of soul and perceptive insights and new images that are released by these "collective phenomena." Here again I would differ from Jung because he probably would not value collective movements as having any value at all for the soul. Long ago, when I was beginning to do my control cases, I dreamed of sitting in a chair on the corner of the main street, Atlantic Avenue, of my home town doing therapy. I was very ashamed of that dream. I thought of Jung in his tower and his quiet library room on the lake and Freud in the room in Vienna. Now I am delighted, proud of that dream.

L.P. *If your psyche does therapy on main street, then don't you want to get people in touch with reality?*

J.H. It's all reality. Why call one section of life "reality"? That's the beauty of the little dream: of course it's just main street, a place in a collective Monopoly game, it's also "Atlantic"—and that's big, and it's Atlantis, and that's even bigger, and submerged and Platonic, so there's all sorts of "reality." It's not serving ice-cream-sodas on main street or cutting hair at a barber shop, it's *doing analysis,* out in the open, but that doesn't mean naive reality. My job is mainly to get people in touch with *psychic* reality, that's the chair I'm in. And anyway, isn't it psychic reality that messes up what you are calling "reality," our sense of reality? That "messing up" is really the psyche trying to penetrate, trying to twist, to re-vision reality so that it is less naive and more psychological.

L.P. *I'd like you to go back to feminism as therapeutic. I'd like you to say more about it.*

J.H. Feminism and femininity is a desperate topic. I steer clear of it. Once you see the whole world in terms of gender you close your mind in a set of blinders, caught in a pair of opposites, and you lose the particular person, like you, in front of me, who happens to be of the female gender. People, you, are far more than female or male. I lose you, the person there, if I reduce you to a supposed feminine essence. Maybe if we used the full vocabulary of psychological traits that were laid out in 1935 by two Harvard psychologists—there were some nineteen thousand traits, that described a personality. Only some of those words are gender words. Having to do with external gender characteristics, psychosexual characteristics, sociogender characteristics . . . of course, I am taking a lot of this from an essay my wife wrote, "The Dogma of Gender"—an excellent essay. She really got to new ground. Where were we?

L.P. *Gender words.*

J.H. Yes, there may be only a few hundred such words out of thousands. Besides that, there are thousands of things about you that have *nothing to do with gender.* If I put you into your gender, I have made a racist move. It's like putting you into being Italian or putting you into being a certain age or a certain class. I have lost you in a sociological category. So I don't want to answer any questions about the feminine, feminism, or so on. I will talk about certain structures of consciousness that have been called feminine and what happens when they are called feminine; we can talk about hysteria or about Dionysus, because Dionysus was considered a Lord or God of women, and the way that works. But I don't want to speak of "the feminine" in a literal sense. These structures of consciousness that we call feminine are in men and are in women and are in neither. They are structures of consciousness. Archetypal patterns, that appear again and again. This touches only tangentially the social problems of women being oppressed—not being paid equal wages, for instance. That's a basic social economic problem. It should be dealt with. It must be dealt with. Or certain laws about property. Or inheritance laws and women. Or with the reluctance of organizations to employ women. Or the Church to let women be priests. There are all sorts of social prejudices. Those need to be dealt with. No question.

But let's not get confused between dealing with those things and defining some kind of consciousness as female or feminine. As my wife says in her paper, either feminists say there are no gender differences and I can climb a telephone pole and shoot a gun and drive a truck just the same as any man (they're assuming already that driving a truck or climbing a telephone pole is male; it's already set up that way), or feminists take the other position and say, the feminine is different. It belongs to the moon, it has to do with instinct and nature and womb and menstruation and breasts and a mode of being that a man doesn't understand. They identify with a particular archetypal pattern, a lunar constellation, say, and define that as "the feminine." In both of those situations the individuality of the woman is trapped in being either nonfeminine or all-feminine; and both the ideas of what's feminine are *stereotypes.*

Psyche, you see, tends to ignore that gender question, curiously enough. Just like the psyche tends to ignore a lot of the questions that the ego thinks are important and identifies with. The psyche doesn't really know in its dream whether you're rich or poor. It doesn't know whether you went to grade school or to college. It doesn't know whether you're a man or a woman. It doesn't know—when I say it doesn't know this, I mean the material it presents in a dream ignores it. I'm handed a written dream. I can't tell if that dream is dreamed by a man or a woman necessarily. I can't tell if that dream is dreamed by somebody twenty or sixty or eighty. I don't know if the dreamer is a city person or a country person, because a city person can have extraordinary dreams about landscapes and rivers. And a country person can be in the middle of a city, because the city is an eternal image and the country is an eternal image, not a sociological or geographical place only. One can be anywhere in one's dreams. I can be in a Greek landscape or I can be in a Scandinavian forest and I may never have been either in Greece or Scandinavia. So the psyche tends to ignore the categories that social psychology organizes things into. It's like married or unmarried, mother or not mother, and so on. In dreams men breast feed and women have penises. Why not?

You can always take a dream and reduce it to sociological categories; but the dream as phenomenon seems not to care about that. Just like it doesn't seem to care about life and death that much. You can have death dreams when you're young and right in the middle of life—a whole series of dreams which seem to be quite clear that you are dying of cancer or that you will die on a certain date. I had such dreams: I was supposed to die on a certain date, and it was as real as it could be. On the other hand, I've worked with people who have died in analysis, and the dreams never made it clear when they would die or even if they would die. Maybe I was too dense to see. . . . Anyway, the idea that dreams have a sexual origin, of course, would then say dreams have a gender origin, and that men's dreams must be different from women's dreams because their sexual organs are different and their chromosomes are different and so on. A dream—I'm sitting in my home on the edge of my bed, and Marybelle in a light blue dress comes in with a bunch of tulips, and I put my arms around her. End of dream. Whose dream is that? A man's dream or a woman's dream? If it's a woman's dream, Mary Bell is still the child from childhood bringing into my reception a chance to meet this child again. And the same thing is true for a man's dream. You can't immediately say the man has an infantile sexuality. But who hasn't—thank God! But what would deprive a woman of having an infantile sexuality, too, with Marybelle? No reason—unless you start off with prejudices. So the sexual origin is not only theoretically questionable, but it leads also to gender thinking. It gives you two problems at once! And it prevents you from just being with that girl who's just walked in the room in the dream. Because you're starting off by categorizing it somewhere. But psyche ignores all that.

5 A RUNNING ENGAGEMENT WITH CHRISTIANITY

L.P. *Strangely enough for a Jungian psychologist, you have mostly avoided discussion of Christian myths. The only ones you have discussed are the betrayal of Jesus and the suffering pathologized Christ. Why?*

J.H. Talking of Christianity in a Christian culture is always a risky business. . . . Partly, I am careful with Christianity because I feel a great deal of respect toward the religion of my fellows; partly, though, I have so much deep-seated animosity that I suppress myself. You know Freud, too, avoided the Christian problem. It's not in his writings. He created other myths, but he doesn't come to terms with the Christian question except to say that all religion is illusion, a sublimated neurosis. He puts aside the content of Christianity . . . very wise, very discreet . . . and yet the entire field he opened up, the repressed, can hardly be talked about without facing the Christian culture, the collective attitudes of Christianity that made this repression. I mean look at the Church and the repression of sexuality. Imagine a culture whose main God-image has no genitals and whose Mother is sexually immaculate, whose Father did not sleep with his Mother. This is a collective image, a *représentation collective* that rules the culture and leaves a psychological heritage: psychologists have to deal with it. Freud tried to deal with it but not directly, not culturally, not in terms of Christianity. Jung tried to deal with it directly; he spent his whole life struggling with Christianity. He worked on the repression by extending Christianity downward into Mercurius, earth, matter, shadow.

L.P. *How do you deal with it?*

J.H. I try to bypass the Christian view by stepping behind it to the Greeks, to polytheism. I have tried to pick up again that great battle between the pagans and the Christians. That battle is not a dead issue at all: it goes on every day inside our Western psyche. What we now call the unconscious are the old Gods returning, assaulting, climbing over the walls of the ego.

L.P. *You want to view the breakdown in the culture and in the individual as a breakdown of Christian structures or a breaking through of more antique cultural structures into modern Western consciousness.*

J.H. I don't want the Christian structures simply to break down. That would just be anarchy or simple anti-Christianism. No, it's more freeing the mythical basis of the psyche from the Christian interpretation of the myths. What made our modern consciousness Christian happened mainly because, as the Christian theologians said, their method of interpretation took each thought "a prisoner for Christ," that is, gave every myth, every fantasy, every image a Christian meaning. So, the big job is to free the psychological material from those Christian meanings. One way to do this might be to show that these images can carry meanings *outside* of the Christian approach, outside of the dogma that already says what they mean. I tried to do this in the image of the pathologized Christ—suffering can mean other things besides resurrection. But Christianity has nailed suffering to resurrection—first nail: it is good for you; second nail; it is isolating and heroic, and third, it always leads to a better day, Easter. Well, it doesn't—we all know that! Suffering has other models, too, like deepening in the sense of Saturn, like dissolving and letting go in the sense of Dionysus, like raging and fighting back; it can make for prophesy; it can make for love; or the kinds of suffering we see in the women in Greek drama. We need many models, besides the Christian one, to locate our psychological experiences.

L.P. *That would be what you call "the return to Greece."*

J.H. The return to Greece means getting out from under the Christian overlay. For instance, I've been looking at some of the mythological structures like the Underworld to show that they can be imagined altogether differently from the Christian viewpoint. That viewpoint makes the Underworld into Hell and Pan into the devil, Hecate into a witch, and the *diamones,* or protective personifications that guided even Socrates, into demons. I'm not in a position to deal with Christianity head on in a theological manner, that is, to examine Christology, to examine Church history, the doctrines, and so forth and so on. I don't know enough theology. All I can do is see the effects of bits of it here and there and to look at all these doctrines, all these ideas, these extraordinary fantasies as acts of imagination, as psychological events. That's what Jung did, except that he was still trying to "save Christianity" as heretics are really. He was still a Christian. I don't have that apologetic burden.

L.P. *Jung validated Christianity by placing different themes of it, like the Trinity, like the Mass, against a wider mythological background. He connected the cross with the worldwide motif of the mandala, the fourfold structure of wholeness.*

J.H. I don't mean that method of anthropological, cross-cultural evidence for Christianity. That's comparative religion. That's fine for validating Christian ideas as archetypal structures. I mean something more like what David Miller does in theology. Have you seen his book *Christs*? Notice that plural ending! He says, "Okay, start with the fundamental Christian writings which are written in the Greek language and you will see in them and through them the pagan myths at work right in the words, and then you deepen Christian fundamentalism into its polytheistic and pagan background." He shows that Christianity is loaded with forgotten meanings. It's full of soul, he says. He shows the clown in Christ and the drunk in Christ and not only the hero myth. This opens a whole new way out—but, it's still theology, apologetics, still committed to saving Christianity, and I want something even more psychological. I am more worried about the actual shadow of Christianity working in our mind-sets, in our repressions, right in the middle of psychology itself. The Christian heritage is constantly at work, like a vaccine, like a toxin, invisibly inside our feelings and reactions and ideas, preventing us from seeing ourselves and our world. A self-deception. Look, why was it necessary for Jung—or Nietzsche or Kierkegaard—to spend a whole life working over Christianity or for Freud to invent whole new myths like the primal horde and that roly-poly polymorphous child of sexuality and the three Invisible Persons of the psyche: Ego, Id, Superego? They were trying to find ways out of the Christian overlay. It will take us ten hours of talking just to go around the very outside of this huge issue of the effect of the Christian two thousand years on the individual case that one meets in psychology. You and me, too, we can't help but be Christian.

L.P. *We are not practicing Christians. . . .*

J.H. Yes, we are, because we are behaving Christians, we behave Christianity—we suffer in a Christian way, we judge in a Christian way, we regard ourselves in a Christian way. We have to see this or we remain unconscious, and that means our unconsciousness is primarily Christianity. Psychotherapy can't move anything, anybody anywhere, until it sees this Christian unconsciousness and that is why Freud had to attack religion and Jung had to try to move Christianity. Even Lacan has said if religion triumphs, and he thinks it will, it would be the end of psychoanalysis.

L.P. *So your work must fight religion?*

J.H. No, not at all! It fights the unconsciousness, the blindness that all myth creates about itself. You never can see the actual myth you are in or only through a glass darkly. I see my work as a long-running engagement with Christianity, a continuing skirmish with the accepted modes of Western thought and therefore with Christian thought, a running engagement all the way through, whether it's in suicide or emotion or Pan and Dionysus or whether it's in the attempt to revalue what was called in alchemy "the primary material" or individual syndromes that have been judged and condemned. It's to save the phenomenon from that organization of the mind which makes our culture sick: belief, unity, truth, identity, integration—all those highly valued words which have a monotheistic psychology behind them.

L.P. *Go on about monotheism.*

J.H. The monotheistic structure creates one trouble after another for patients. Take their own history, for example. Our monotheistic tradition literalizes history into facts. History was not a familiar fantasy to the Greeks or to most polytheistic cultures—high or low. But for the Christians everything comes with a date. Dig it up, prove the historical Jesus, treasure the documents, the relics . . . nail it with a date. This obsession with historical facts makes everyone's personal story into a history of literal facts. We behave as Christians when we believe that facts determine us: I am crazy because this and this happened in the past—my mother didn't hold me against her breast, my father exposed himself to me. Dig up the historical facts. But I could be crazy because my soul is "away," traveling, or because it is an initiation rite or because a daimon has come to me with some new demands or because there is a turn in the story that doesn't make sense now since it's only on page 75, but toward page 245, when I'm sixty years old, then I'll see what the craziness is about. We call such explanations "crazy superstitions"—only the facts of history are allowed to determine us. That's Christian historical thinking, and we believe these stories by calling them facts. This bears directly on the literal way most psychology takes case histories.

L.P. *I have read your essay "On the Fiction of Case History" (1975) which is now in your new book* Healing Fiction *(1982). There you say that Freud wasn't seriously historical because he knew that the historical memories of his patients were "invented" facts. Freud wasn't historical because he was psychological. His case histories have to be read as a new style, a new genre of literature which tells a story in the "case-history mode."*

J.H. Now Freud was Jewish and, I think, when he made that discovery about his patients inventing the "facts" in their memories and he used a Biblical metaphor, "Tell it not in Gath . . . ," he was putting himself in touch with the Jewish approach to the facts of history.

L.P. *What's that—is it different from the Christian? I thought the Jews "invented" history and that Christianity took its historicism from Judaism.*

J.H. Even those words bother me: Judaism and Christianity. Why are all the other religions called *isms*—Buddhism, Taoism— but Christianity—that's special, that's not an ism . . .

L.P.   *But what about the Jewish approach to history?*

J.H.   ... even the Greek and Roman religions became "paganism." The Greeks didn't have a word "religion." Christianity just didn't know what to do with its Greek inheritance—so they baptized it "pagan." It means "rocky hill": I'm pagan; Man of the Hill!

L.P.   *What about that Jewish approach to history?*

J.H.   Freud made a Jewish move with his case history: he deliteralized it. The Jewish approach is the *story* and the variations on the story. History is a series of images, tales, geographies, figures, lessons. It's not so much fact. Psychologically, it's the story of Christ, not the historical Christ—the redeemer is in imagination, in the imaginal, always about to appear, but never phenomenal. In fact, you could say the redeemer is the imagination itself. Like Blake said, "Jesus the Imagination," but then he was a Kabbalist. As far as I know, is it a Jewish mode to prove the historical Abraham, the historical Noah, the historical David? It's certainly a Christian mode to dig up evidence for the historical Christ. Some of the very finest, most subtle minds—Renan, Schweitzer—have been engaged in this ridiculous business of proving or disproving their religion with historical "facts." I don't think the Jewish mode thinks in terms of scientific evidence to show the uniqueness of its faith.

L.P.   *There's the literal evidence, the Bible, the texts....*

J.H.   But the story isn't literalized into a credo, a dogma that must be believed.

L.P.   *It only has to be retold....*

J.H.   It has to be retold, that's the whole business of the Midrash, it has to be retold and it has to be twisted—like what we said about Bach, that he left no form as he found it, he had to make his own twist to the form that he got—to my mind that's Jewish thinking.

L.P.   *Jewish thinking often seems "twisted" to Christians. Freud, for instance.*

J.H. But you're not deliberately twisting things, just to be perverse. It's more that in order to give a story a new twist, you have to be in touch with your own pathology because that's where the twist comes from. To be true to the story doesn't mean not to twist it. It means don't forget to tell the story. But not always in the same way, with the same meaning: that's just fundamentalism, sticking to the exact same version, word for word without any twist. Now the Greeks and the Jews have a similarity: the Greeks say that the only form of impiety is to neglect or forget the Gods, and it seems to me that the Jewish concern with neglecting or forgetting God shows not just in all the orthodox rules, but it shows very importantly in not forgetting to tell the story. Like Passover: "Why is this night different from all other nights?" The whole story has to be told again, in every detail, all the images, even the taste of bitter herbs, and the pathological horrors with little twists depending on the teller.

L.P. *I think your notion of Christian monotheism is really Christian fundamentalism. It's a strange thing for us in Italy where we have a very long tradition of being Christian in an almost detached way . . . belief isn't the point. Nor is the text, the literal statements, the historical facts. A "good Christian" for us doesn't have to read the "good book," as you call it in America. Besides, there is a long Christian tradition of reading the Bible as having four levels of truth, not just one, the literal fundamentalist sense.*

J.H. I like to think that allegorical style, playing with the words and twisting the meanings, begins with a Jew, with Philo of Alexandria, who was very Greek, too. But you are right, I do equate Christianism with moralistic fundamentalism. I think you have to face this level of Christianism because that's where its real strength, its world-conquering force, lies. It's not Christian love that's conquered the world; it's not its sophisticated interpretations, sophisticated theology. It's successful because it mobilizes the will, and the will needs fundamentalism or it doesn't know what to do.

Fundamentalism serves the hero myth. It gives you fundamental principles—words, truths, directions. It builds a strong ego. It is American psychology. No Hermes, no Dionysus, no Aphrodite

in it at all. Utterly monotheistic because there is only one meaning, one reading of the text—like, for instance, the one meaning
of Christ's suffering. Another one of these monotheistic disasters
of psychology is the unity fantasy. Oh, you can argue that Christianity wasn't really monotheistic, that it is trinitarian or even
pluralistic, the three persons and Mary and all the saints—very
true—but still the basic idea is the one and only Catholic Church,
the one true religion, the historical cosmic Christ, the one and
only Son of God, therefore anything that doesn't fit within that
unity is split, or schizoid, a hysterical complex or autonomous or
whatever else, and you have lost the fact that you are a bundle of
many levels, people, noises, impulses, trends, personalities, possibilities and no two days are the same and no two voices are the
same and one is a loose structure of many beings—Jung called
them complexes.

But as long as one lives in the myth of unity one is forced into
commanding the psyche to obey the principle of unity and the
unifier, the ego, creating this monstrous Western ego, which then
has to be subdued by all kinds of Christian virtues: tolerance,
self-control, patience, humility, charity, obedience, poverty . . . all
this huge ascetic structure to deal with the Monster which is created by its own dogma! The Greeks also had the problem of the
monstrous ego: their culture had the problem of *hubris,* it belongs to the human nature, but they didn't need that kind of
systematic asceticism that you have in the Christian culture. So
that the repression which Freud placed at the basis of our relation
with the unconscious is nothing more than the Christian myth at
work in us each, cutting us off from our innate polytheistic imagination and renaming it, the unconscious.

L.P. *This monstrous Western ego that has to be subdued appears
in Jungian psychology where it must be relativized to the self in
the process of individuation. Jung writes of the self as the God-
image and compares it with Christ. Is your resistance to discussing the self in your writings a further example of your resistance
to Christianity?*

J.H. The self idea may have come to Jung from his own experience or from his study of Eastern religions—Atman, Brahman—

or from his patients or German mystics or alchemy—it doesn't matter how he arrived at the idea. What matters is that it has become amalgamated with Christology and monotheistic unity because we are in a Christian culture. So when Jungians use the term "self" they can't help but be in the old monotheistic senex structure of unity and centering. The self idea doesn't get us out of the trap, it closes us back into it. It's a hopeless circle of hoping to get out of the ego and into the self, via what the Jungians call "the ego-self axis." But what is that axis? The Catholic Church knows: it's the saints, it's Mary, it's the daimones and figures and voices, the *anima mundi.* So I spend my time examining the *anima mundi,* which is not an axis but a pleroma, a great fullness of psychic realities . . . full of the unexpected. . . . In which the ego and the self are heroes or archons or fictions or complexes, with their different styles of rhetoric, persuasion. Unfortunately, Jungian psychology has got itself caught by its rhetoric. It really believes in these "things," these hypostases, ego and self, which are abstract concepts to begin with and not images and figures, so they are talking *theology* and not psychology. Jungian theology has taken these two luminaries in the field of psychic realities as the two Great Stars and drawn an imaginary line between them called "the axis" and has tried to skew the vast panoply of heavens and hells to rotate around this one axis. Isn't this familiar to you? Doesn't this remind you of Christian theology and the *axis mundi* of Christ, the mediator between man and God? The Christian culture cannot help but put even the newest visions, like Jung's, right back into the same mold. That's why I try to stand on the pagans, on the Greeks, because they were constantly skirmishing with the Christian *Weltanschauung.* It keeps one conscious of the Christian traps.

L.P. *You struggle so hard to maintain the "new" against the "old." Perhaps Jungian theology, as you call it, is the new within the old. Perhaps it is a mode of revitalizing the Christian culture and that the Jungian movement in the long run will be seen as a branch of Protestantism as you yourself have suggested.*

J.H. It's already happened. Jung has already been taken a "prisoner for Christ." Jungian psychology now is a *Heilsweg,* a path of salvation, and, if Lacan is right, then Jungian psychology, because it's now a religion, has stopped being psychological. No, I don't think the turn to Jung to revitalize Christianity is right, not right for Christianity either. As far as religion goes, it seems better to me to read *Job* than Jung's *Answer to Job* or to go to Mass than to read Jung about it.

L.P. *The value of Jung here is that he opened Christianity again as a myth. He opened up its psychological importance—just exactly what you try to do with the Greek myths.*

J.H. It's not at all the same! It's a matter of *which* myths you are opening up. Greek myths bring Greek consciousness, the entire project of know-thyself. They bring psychology. They bring a subtle awareness of the complications of life because of all the Gods and Goddesses. And they bring dimensions Christianity doesn't want to deal with, really, like Aphrodite, like Hades, like Mars. . . . Christianism means simplicity, trust, childlikeness. Don't get too fancy. Ignorance is all right as long as you believe. Don't even read the Bible too much, say the Catholics. Don't interpret too much, say the Protestants. Luther said those allegorical interpretations were "whores," you can use them any way you want. And your own Bishop of Milan, Ambrose, Doctor of the Church, Teacher of Augustine, saint, said we are born to believe, not inquire.

Christianity doesn't require consciousness at all. I am afraid of it. In my bones, I am afraid of Christian unconsciousness, because, unlike Buddhism, say, or even Judaism, Christianism lives myths deliberately, insisting they are not myths, and this has dreadful paranoid consequences. We see it in the ego-self axis: this is a mythical fiction, but it is presented as empirical fact. It imputes meaning as if it were scientifically objectively known to what is inherently unknown and unexpected—"the unconscious." Then this system justifies its view of meaning by saying that the self is the archetype of meaning and the deepest human need is for meaning. A circular argument—of course, the rhetoric of the self must speak in circles because that is its self-description: a circle; then, too, it incorporates the unexpected into its circularity, by calling it synchronicity. Nothing can escape; that's frightening because it's a paranoid way of proceeding, and as you know, paranoia is a disorder of meaning, according to the textbooks.

L.P. *This implies that psychic reality does not fit into any single pattern of meaning. Yet I know you're not saying that everything is meaningless. More likely you are saying that unlike Jung's psychology, yours does not rely only on the self idea for meaning. Meaning, for you, seems to live in phenomena rather than in any kind of subjectivity.*

J.H. I am trying to say that psychic reality is unexpected, inventive, unforeseen—just like our dreams—and that the meaning given by the self idea is no longer unexpected. People already know what to expect from the self: it's already conceptualized. As Adolf Guggenbühl says, it's already become "smooth": fourfold mandalas, synchronicities, transpersonal experiences. Self experiences, and the idea of the self, can very well be defenses, new paranoid pathologies. I get very suspicious when people talk of their religious experiences in this self rhetoric. It's too conventional, too smooth.

L.P. *So when you write that Homer should be in every hotel bedroom rather than the Bible, you mean that the Bible is already too well known. It might have been in your day but . . .*

J.H. It still is in the basic American fundamentalist culture. Besides it's not the literal Greeks versus the literal Bible in the literal hotel room. It's not that I am against Christianity or against the self. It's that to work with psychic realities in your life you just can't put the new wine back into old bottles. The things that Freud and Jung uncovered are so precious that to lose them again in the great maw of the two-thousand-year-old Christian dragon feels terrible to me. I think that's the emotion Lacan must feel when he concludes that religion will win out and put an end to psychoanalysis.

L.P. *Your image there comes from the hero myth.*

J.H. When you go on the Christian stage, you begin to talk in that rhetoric. We are in the Christian fairy tale now, trying to save the soul from the old king. And I don't want to be in this tale. It makes the soul too precious and makes the analyst into a heroic ego and makes the tradition only negative. The whole thing gets set up wrong. That's why I don't use any of this language in my work.

L.P.   *What else "don't you use"? I mean what further can you say about the effect of Christianity on the individual case?*

J.H.   Another Christian bias one has to meet constantly in psychology is the notion of evil. Again, in the Greek world there was no particular principle of evil, there was no Devil; evil was not separated in that way from good. There was ignorance, and there was ugliness, and so on and so forth, in Socratic thinking, but every single God has a mode of being destructive. Dionysus could be the liberator and Dionysus could be the destroyer and, what's more, the two sides might be going on *at the same time.* Can you imagine for one moment Christ the Saviour also being Christ the Destroyer? Both. That the God of Love might also be a killer? Both. Like Dionysus or Apollo or Aphrodite. That's intolerable for us. The Christian mind can't admit, can't allow, a destructive possibility co-present or co-terminous, as they used to say, with love and goodness and salvation. Christianism has to use defense mechanisms and deny and split and project the destructive aspect onto the enemy—the heathens, the Jews, the Catholics, the Reformers, the terrorists. . . . And then it tries to get the part back it has split from, by converting it or loving the enemy or turning the other cheek. It's trapped in its own defense mechanism. It's made a dogma of splitting, which it glorifies as "The Problem of Evil." Now the Greek mind was subtle enough to see that things aren't split. Everything is mixed. There is no good and evil, or rather there is good-*and*-evil, because shadow goes on everywhere and isn't a separate principle. But Christianity likes the childish mind, it is a religion of the child archetype, so it stresses being simple, which means originally being single not subtle. Christianity wants a "single-eyed" vision—Paul, or is it Jesus himself, who says that? This separates the destructive side out and sets it up as an independent idea called "evil." Then the individual person begins to see pieces of himself as evil, and he separates them from parts called good. Repression. The shadow, and so on and so forth.

The patient is constantly asking himself what is wrong, what he should be guilty about, trying to correct himself—get rid of the evil—instead of just paying attention to what is actually going on in detail the way you would with any phenomenon in nature. A great big wave pounding the surf: it's not good, it's not evil. You just look at it, feel it, ride it, or step back. Say you come across a fox in the forest: you'd stand very still and watch it. You start off with curiosity, interest, amazement, enjoyment—but the notion of evil makes you step away from what is happening. You say, Is this a good omen or an evil one, is this a good dream or a bad one, was it right what I did or wrong? And then you have stopped being attentive to the image, what is actually happening, and you are inside your mind doing a subjective examination of motives. You are back in the ego and have left the fox altogether. Guilt always reinforces the ego, it's the neatest defense mechanism the ego has. Under the guise of attacking yourself and humbling yourself, you are back in the old ego of the Christian culture looking at psyche through moral glasses.

L.P. *You have made that point about the phenomenological approach rather than the moralistic approach in your writings on suicide, masturbation, masochism—the shadow side that we talked about earlier. Now you seem to be saying that the Christian attitude doesn't allow for a phenomenological approach.*

J.H. Exactly! It doesn't let you just look at things. We are still in the Middle Ages when the workmen who carved the images on the cathedrals were told what they could and could not carve. Christianity has already declared what all the images mean in its language of good and evil. Psychology can't look at things through the glasses of evil: you can't see what might be going on in the suicide or the masturbation or the masochism. . . .

L.P. *Aren't you missing the depth of the shadow that the Christian idea of evil is pointing to?*

J.H. That's the Christian argument right there! "Ah, my son, you have no notion of the wiles of the Devil. He always makes you think he isn't there—we have to watch for him all the time." Bullshit. The Greeks and lots and lots of other polytheistic cultures had and have intense perception of depth, of the wiles of the Gods, of the seeds of destruction everywhere—without having a moralistic stance. It's not the Devil I object to—in fact the Devil is the last mythical personification left in Christianity—they got rid of the saints who weren't historical, but nobody is trying to dig up the historical devil—it's not the Devil that's the problem, it's the moral glasses that you put on your nose with the pretension that you can see much more acutely that way. We can't really see the psyche with those spiritual glasses.

L.P.   *That, too, is one of your main arguments against Christianity, I mean that its bias toward spirit distorts or empties the soul.*

J.H.   It sounds very dogmatic to say that Christianity is against the soul, and I've written about that in so many different ways that it's not only sounding dogmatic but it's getting tedious. Still, Christian thinking has been primarily an expression of the spirit, not an expression of the body and not an expression of the soul, and it even opposes the spirit to the soul; therefore in the New Testament we have very little about dreams, we have very little about soul phenomena, and a great deal about spirit phenomena: speaking in tongues, conversions, missions, healing, miracles, preaching. The word "psyche" outnumbers "pneuma" by a huge score. The soul as the middle ground between body and spirit got squeezed out and with it went all the richness of what Christianism called paganism. Nowadays we can't tell soul from spirit: they both have become white cloudy immaterial notions opposed to the body and tangible matter. We are so immersed in the materialist viewpoint which Christianity itself brought about, that soul and spirit look just alike. A psychology that starts out from Christianity becomes spiritualized, a spirit psychology, a spiritual theology. Soul enters only via symptoms, via outcast phenomena like the imagination of artists or alchemy or "primitives," or of course, disguised as psychopathology. That's what Jung meant when he said the Gods have become diseases: the only way back for them in a Christian world is via the outcast.

L.P.   *Then the medical model of dealing with psychopathology, treating it to cure the patient of it, would be, in your view, a*

*further example of Christian suppression of the Gods in the dis-
eases.*

J.H.   Yes.

L.P.   *What are some other effects of Christianity on the individual case?*

J.H.   Well, take the problem of *belief.* The Greeks didn't have to
believe in their Gods. They didn't say, "I believe in. . . ." That
came in with Christianity. They didn't have a theology—they
had myths. And we need to read our psychic life not theological-
ly but mythically. They didn't even have a word for religion.
When something appears—a voice, an image, a dream—you respond to it. If Marybelle comes in, like we were talking about a
while back, a pagan responds to her. But a Christian has to ask, Is
this from God or the Devil? Is it real or did I make it up? Do I
believe in this figure, and if I believe, then what are the grounds
of my belief? and so on and so forth. This disturbs the natural
relationship with phenomena. The very act of believing, the dec-
laration of "I believe," is a subjectivism. It cuts one off from
what's there. It cuts one off from imagination, from one's animal
reality. As if we could make something real or true by believing
in it. If your faith is fervent enough. . . . That locates reality in a
wishing ego—for who does this believing, who affirms the reality
of the voice or the God or Maribel? "I" do! That is a shameful
way to go about things. It's fundamentally antireligious because it
is insensitive to the reality of what is there.

L.P.   *If the Christian idea of belief cuts us off from our reactions
or damages the animal, why is it you have several times, while
we are talking, used such phrases as "it's part of my faith" when
you are making a strong statement? Isn't this a statement of belief, and aren't you showing that belief, whether you like the
word or not, is inescapable?*

J.H.   If I think about it, probably, faith means to me an unreflected way of going about things. It's something like style. And it's
also something like deep passion, an archetypal propulsion that
comes from principles. Now these principles . . . I don't see them

as "articles of faith"—that is, formulated belief structures, doctrines.

L.P. *Why aren't they just opinions then?*

J.H. Maybe they are—but the emotion that propels them seems, well . . . tribal, ancestral, animal. I have been writing recently about "animal faith"—an idea taken from George Santayana—which is that faith in the world: that it is there, that it won't give way underfoot when you take the next step, that you just know which way to turn and how to proceed. It's the faith your hands have and your feet have.

L.P. *And your heart? That's where Christian faith is "located." It implies a love in connection with the object of that faith.*

J.H. Must we have an "object" of faith—isn't that belief, again? Animal faith, or what I'm trying to get at, of course, has love in it, and hatred, too; it starts in the feet and hands. The heart is the right place for faith if we were still a classical culture where the heart was the place of sensing, of a blood-soul, like an animal, or of imagining. But now because of the Christians again, Augustine especially, the heart has become the place of personal confession and self-examination and conscience . . . subjectivism . . . But the hands and feet are still uncontaminated: the cat jumps on the tree and starts climbing. The tree is not an object of faith to which the cat gives assent. It is a tree in an ecological field belonging to the cat's climbing. The cat has an *animal* faith in the tree and it loves the tree, loves itself, loves jumping and climbing—no self-examination there, no introspection about belief. Or it would stay home; or see a priest . . .

L.P. *. . . or an analyst.*

J.H. . . . that cat lives its belief in what psychology calls avoidance behavior. It tends to move around a suspicious object. It sniffs, it has its ears up, on the ready. It's superstitious. So, the kind of belief I want to explore and that Christianism abhors is superstition. That's where the *diamones*—what Jung called the little people—are very much alive. We feel their power in all sorts of little avoidance behaviors, little superstitions, little rituals, little secret neurotic compulsions. Superstitions keep the world alive for us—ladders might fall, cats bring bad luck. But not just these collective superstitions: I mean your own private ones about your bed, about the night, about your diet ... wherever there is something a little uncanny, just outside the borders of consciousness. Superstitions bring you special reports. They are your foreign correspondents from the alien people across the borders. Animals live superstitiously, ritually. But animals also live instinctually. What does that mean? Doesn't it mean that animals live in a world alive, receiving messages? This is animism as the anthropologists call it. But what is animism? It's *esse in anima.* It's living in the world via the soul and sensing the soul in the world ... feeling the world as personified, as emotional, as saying something. Christianity can't abide superstition because it has "overcome" animism, and it has codified all its superstitions into true belief, the belief in the one true Christ, and that move represses your inherent religiosity in relation to the world, your relation to powers beyond you that humble the ego. For Christianity the world is dead, only dead matter. Ladders aren't alive. Christianity is utterly materialistic, and animals too aren't allowed souls, because, if they were, then that would lead to ladders, matter, too, having soul. But cats aren't materialists; they are Neoplatonists. They live in the *anima mundi,* in a world full of figures, omens, signatures. They live avoidance behaviors—just like Socrates, who listened to his daimon telling him what to avoid. But—if you ask, "Tell me, Dr. Hillman, do you really believe walking under a ladder brings bad luck?" Oh, no, of course I don't *believe* it. I don't give it reasoned assent. I don't *stand* for it in that Christian sense of Protestant ego—commitment, ego responsibility. But I may follow my avoidance behavior. I act superstitious—and don't let "belief" interfere. Superstitions depend on the moment; they stay ambiguous, and so they keep in touch with our instantaneous feelings, instincts.

The Christian kind of belief cuts us off from our reactions: it commands them. And then, because we are cut off, we have to be saved, redeemed. Maybe Christianity is right not to be concerned with the souls of animals. Animals don't need saving—except ecologically from humans, including Christian humans. Christianity works very hard at saving the soul, but this seems impossible if it leaves out the animal soul. This extraordinary religion, the religion that we are all in no matter how hard we try to deny it or escape it, has lost its animals. So it is always fulfilling its image of a God without genitals, without animals, no matter how much it tries to save the soul. Christianity wouldn't have to moralize about the soul so much and worry about evil so much, about belief so much, if it didn't have something in its basic archetypal fantasy, inherently in the religion itself, that is destructive to the soul. And that is why psychoanalysis is engaged with Christianity. It has to be. Psychoanalysis has to be worried about, superstitious about, the shadow of Christianity and its effect on the soul. Psychology's job is always with the shadow—"the horror, the horror"—and Christianity says the soul is saved or will be saved by belief in the Christian fantasy, but the horror, the horror may lie in that very fantasy itself.

6 ON BEING BIOGRAPHICAL

L.P. *Listening to you I am constantly struck by how American you are. You use German words and French and even Italian ones, you refer to European writers and history, but still your mind and your energy, the way you view Europe, is still to me very American.*

J.H. I came to Europe right after the war, in 1946, and was educated here—in Paris, in Ireland, in Switzerland . . . my first wife was European, my four children are very European. . . . I am a Swiss citizen now, but still the cultural soul, I guess we can call it that, is American. My animal soul is American.

L.P. *There is a tradition of "European" Americans—Cooper, Twain, Henry James, Eliot, Pound, Gertrude Stein . . .*

J.H. Writers. But psychologists seem to go the other way: they start in Europe and go to America. There just aren't any native American psychologists. Think of it: every single psychological movement has its root in a European figure, even the laboratories, even the minor schools—Erikson, Horney, Fromm, Perls, Marcuse.

L.P. *William James?*

J.H. Very important. But he is not an exception. He spent years in Germany and had a European sort of breakdown, like Freud, like Jung, and was a neurotic, philosophical, European sort of man despite his American pragmatism. America just isn't a psychological place. You have to be immersed in Europe to be psychological.

L.P. *So, even if your cultural soul and your animal soul is American, your intellectual development is European.*

J.H.   The idea of intellectual development is really a critic's idea
or a schoolbook's idea or a biographical idea, it isn't the way the
mind really ... the mind doesn't necessarily work in steps; it fills
out *lacunas,* we become aware because of a *lacuna,* and it's the
lacuna that's hungry and then begins to eat something, passionately eats something, like I ate the Renaissance. Psychopathology
was another hunger. I was trying to see further into it. Or the
whole question of feminine inferiority, Dionysus; I was into that
for a long time. What I didn't read on Dionysus ... collected all
the books that were written in the eighteenth, nineteenth century, Italian books, French books ... and then the question of hysteria. It was a hunger coming out of an unknown part of my own
psyche, out of my *lacuna,* so the *opus* that you work on is part of
the *operare* on yourself, but it isn't a development the way you
go to a museum and study the development of a painter: in 1904
he did this, in 1906 he did that, in 1908 he began to ... that's a
kind of after-the-fact reportage: it doesn't work that way. You
have an embarrassing ignorance and a huge hunger and you fall
into it and afterward you talk of "intellectual development."

L.P.   *There are patterns that follow phases though, if you don't
want to call it development....*

J.H.   Yes, there are patterns like there are patterns in Picasso,
where you see the same artist and model or you see certain
goatheads or you see certain bull motifs again and again through-
out his work—so there would be that kind of pattern. But it
seems to me I stand too close to see such detailed patterns. There
are general themes though, the mythological pattern is certainly
one, yes; the philosophical pattern is one, yes; the clinical pattern
is another one—the constant return to basic syndromes of one
kind or another, and the attempt to keep connections between
mythological figures and those syndromes. But I can't really see
the patterns. Maybe I don't want to look for them.

L.P.   *This seems like your resistance to the interview itself, as if
you don't want really—not expose yourself—but rather you don't
want to know yourself.*

J.H.   Oh, that's very true—if you mean by know yourself give an
account of yourself, report on yourself. I don't believe for a mo-

ment in explanatory biography, in psychobiography. I like the old Greek idea of biography: it just meant what one had been through: "I was at Thermopylae" or "I worked with Praxiteles for a year." What you did, where you were, who you were with. I had a tremendous fight with some friends here in Zurich when I left for America a couple of years ago. Half a dozen friends; and we met every month or so, and they said, "Why are you going to Dallas?" And they began to tell me why and I got enraged. I don't believe in that question, Why? I don't believe there are answers to the question, Why? When I'm dead, I said, you can find out why I moved to Dallas. Because you can read backward from what happened later in my life why I moved there, or you can read forward from what happened earlier in Zurich that made me move, causally. But all that about causes are fictions. Psychobiography. They said something good, though, and this I do think is right. They said that my favorite belief is the belief in uncaused spontaneity, in no answers to why! They are pretty good psychologists, these friends, and Jungians too!

L.P. *How did you first find Jungian psychology?*

J.H. The first person from whom I heard the name Jung was an American friend who had had a breakdown. He was about three or four years older, we were in Europe together in 1946–47, we went to Prague together, Paris. He was in Jungian analysis in London, and he was painting, psychological paintings; a very disturbed fellow, he died when he was only about thirty, and both he and his mother were in analysis in London. I had no idea of what analysis was, he didn't even talk too much about that, but it seemed immediately to me that analysis had to do with the healing of very sick persons, because this friend was a sick person. Then I met another fellow in Dublin, an American, and he gave me one or two books by Jung to read. Then I was about twenty-two, I was studying psychology, philosophy, and literature, and I read *Psychological Types* and *Modern Man in Search of a Soul*. It didn't do anything special; I wasn't converted or excited. Reading Freud's *Traumdeutung*, when I was twenty, was a revelation. Jung wasn't a revelation; but he did touch something in me that I didn't realize at the time. This friend in Dublin was writing his own dreams down, he was doing his own psychoanalysis, and that impressed me very much: writing your dreams! That was a great idea! So when I got tuberculosis that next year and was in a sanatorium, I began to write my dreams down, too, and I read some more of Jung. Where he touched me was with the idea of individuation—that there was a process going on that one could trust. It became like a mystique of believing in my own fate: a very puer way of understanding Jung, of course! I mean there I was with TB—before there was streptomycin or PAS and people my age dying around me—and I was believing in my own fate!

L.P. *Do you feel that there were strands or moments in your earlier years before you met these friends who mentioned Jung to you, before you came to Europe, that already prepared or indicated that you would come to Jung and depth psychology?*

J.H. Many strands, sure, and they came out in my analysis. But other strands didn't. Analysis follows the dreams, and the dreams aren't very interested in biography. They ignore all sorts of people and places that may have composed most of your life. If you start with the dream, say some childhood dream as in Jung's biography, you begin a very different life story than if you start with what psychiatry calls anamnesis. So there are strands that I never dreamt about, never analyzed, which seem from a biographical viewpoint to be basic . . .

L.P. *"Biographical viewpoint"?*

J.H. . . . I mean my conscious understanding of myself as a historical continuity, as what you asked about "intellectual development." My time in the Navy, 1944–46, when I worked in the hospitals—the work they gave me was with the blind and the maimed and the deaf. I worked nearly entirely with the blind. I was then nineteen years old. So all these blinded people who came back from the battles of the Pacific were put into this one hospital. They had lost their eyes, faces blown away, and so on, and I identified extremely with these people and with the horror of the American system of rehabilitation. We took them to parties, we got them dancing, got them dates, . . . well, reintegration into American life was on the most superficial level imaginable.

It made them drunks. Cheap, cheap. Of course, we also taught them how to walk, to eat, to read, to get dressed and do things, but basically that horror that we see now in a film like *Apocalypse Now,* I saw when I was nineteen years old and I was horrified. . . . But it was more than that. There was bitterness and sentimentalism. I wrote war poems. I had a huge hatred for authorities, the officers, and medical doctors and the social system. But it was more than that, too. What was missing was something deeper. Everything was organized around adaptation, but nothing meant anything, and no one gave us the training, the tools to work with. So I moved from the barracks right into the ward and lived with the patients, which wasn't allowed, but something wanted to go into it more deeply and the only way to go in deeper was to go in closer. I suppose that's American, too, and probably says a lot about American, Californian, feeling-therapy: that personal closeness is an attempt to go deeper in a culture where there are no deep ideas, no structures of depth. Anyway I was already caught up in psychotherapy at nineteen even if I didn't know the word.

L.P. *Couldn't you also say that your social consciousness awoke in the hospital, and if so, it raises an interesting question about the relation between social conscience, even guilt, and psychotherapy. Perhaps one of the urges to do psychotherapy is the urge to do something about collective, social wrongs—not just to help or heal individuals.*

J.H. Perhaps when you are young you take on the world of collective social wrongs in that kind of way. I wasn't conscious of that. I thought the way to take on wrongs was through politics and journalism. That's what I studied first and where my ambition was. When I arrived in Europe in June 1946, I got a job immediately with the American radio and I was a radio newswriter. I wrote about the peace negotiations in Paris, about Molotov, about Palestine, about the occupation in Germany. I actually wrote the news that was broadcast every morning at seven o'clock or in the afternoon, every three hours. I was a kid: imagine the innocence, no knowledge of history, no knowledge of literature, well not much anyway, so incredibly American and right in the middle of bombed-out Germany, in Frankfurt. Again it was a place, like the navy hospital, where there was intense suffering and there was this terrible distortion between the Americans and the condition of Germany. All these ruined people and a society that ignores it or treats it in some freakish way. I guess like Gunther Grass would see it. I always thought that I would be taken off the news desk because I was always seeing through the other journalists who would go to the same press conference and come back and write their stories that I would read on the press services, the AP wire or the UP wire, and they would pick up half a sentence and turn it into a new crisis, a new war, between Russia and the United States, and all this they were doing while the peace conference was going on in Paris. . . . I had been to the same press conference and heard the same words and I didn't see their war angle at all. So I always expected something to happen to me, but nothing did. Nobody cared. I could write what I wanted.

L.P.   *Were you writing for yourself then as well?*

J.H.   Only later, when I moved to Paris. I went there to study and there was a tremendous amount of intellectual activity there then 1947, 1948. And then I think I did wake up . . . I mean specifically that I was dying for intellectual life. It wasn't the university but to be intellectual. That was something an American doesn't know about. If you want to be intellectual, you are academic; and I saw in Paris that you could be intellectual without being academic. I remember one girlfriend saying to me, "If you want to write, what are you studying comparative literature for? Write!" The same thing happened later in Dublin when I could live my literary fantasy. We had a literary review, *Envoy,* and I knew all kinds of writing people, Brendan Behan, Patrick Kavanagh, Myles na Gopaleen . . . J. P. Donleavy, who is still a good friend. But anyway, the whole journalistic side dissolved into what was behind it, writing, simply writing. But being a young American the only right to writing, the only justification for the social conscience you mentioned, was journalistic writing. I couldn't really think of writing itself until I got to Dublin. Or maybe that's why I went to Dublin. The psyche picks its geographies.

L.P.   *When did you go to Zurich?*

J.H.   After Dublin I lived in India for a year or more, when I got more and more neurotic, and I began to study my dreams. Energy was always going away from what I thought I was there for, to write a novel; it was going into myself . . . and I remember going up very high, fourteen thousand feet in the Himalayas, and before I left I had been talking with a guru, Gopi Krishna; so then one afternoon I was over at his place and the heat, Jesus, tremendous heat, and I was sitting on this sticky chair with flies all around, and he said, "Go high in the mountains, that's very good to go high in the mountains, because that's where man meets God." So off we went on the mountains on our ponies, up so high that you can't breathe, you know . . . and I had a nightmare up there. It was a very simple dream, but it was actually a terrifying nightmare. And that was the beginning of coming down, getting down from that mountain, and down and down and down until I got to Zurich. It was a journey of six months or more by the time I got to Zurich and the Jung Institute. That was in February 1953. I had been reading a lot more of Jung in India, but I still couldn't face that I needed analysis. I went to a lecture just to see what it was like. And I remember walking out when it was over saying, "Well, I know this place isn't for me!" So, of course, I stayed there for years and became its director of studies, completely wrapped up in that Institute for almost twenty years!

L.P.   *You didn't go there intending to be an analyst yourself. You went there really as a patient.*

J.H.   Yes. And I've always been suspicious of people who go into "training." For me training was my own mess. I didn't intend at all to be an analyst.

L.P.   *Why?*

J.H.   I didn't think that I was able . . . I didn't want the feeling of being trapped in a little room seeing people all day long. I think I was afraid of the involvement, simply afraid of the whole thing, afraid of the people, afraid of the psyche, afraid of myself, of not knowing, afraid that I wasn't myself in shape to do it, too sick myself. So between March and November 1955 I had dreams and

I had feelings, and things happened, and I began to try. And from the beginning doing analysis meant being not professional. I remember my colleagues, who were beginning at the same time, putting on suits and ties and looking for offices, and I remember that for me it was just the reverse. Even in Dallas today where I'm a professor, I practice sometimes in bare feet. Not on purpose, I mean, I am not trying to make an act. I never have shaved just because a patient is coming. I just go ahead, just as the day is . . . there's something in me that is very antiprofessional. And that was already there in the beginning: I remember one patient's dream, from then, in which she came to a maid's room to do analysis (she was a wealthy German pretentious girl) and the building where I saw people was like a servant's quarters, a sloppy, slummy place. . . . These stories seem so personal. I wish I could let the psyche speak more. The difference between ego and psyche isn't only theoretical; it's in how you tell a story. It's in getting the subjectivity out of it, so the story, the image takes over. Is this the fault of the interview: the first person singular? The fault of biography? Somehow the images get trapped in personalism. . . . Maybe I'm too attached, so that the images can't get free enough of the memories to become really images. I do admire people who have a gift for telling stories about themselves so that they are all imagistic and not so confessional. My landlady in Dublin used to get beaten up and crash around between her husband and her lover all night—the three of them roaring around with fire pokers and banging pots and dishes, and we all stayed in our rooms hearing the whole thing, all the sexual details too—and next morning she'd tell me all about it, "Ah, James . . ." like it was a story utterly free of her. Maybe I was her analyst. Amazing. It's the art of working a biography, and I don't have that art. Besides, as we were saying earlier, I'm a "behaving Christian": I'm prudish about revealing my sexual life, so I don't have that way of making powerful images out of my life.

But there's something else, which is that I believe very much in the anonymity of one's work. The work is anyway anonymous. Who writes the book? Where does all that come from? To start making oneself the author seems pretentious and deadly.

Every time I was asked by a publisher to send a biographical account and a picture I refused. I have never had my picture on any book cover, and I always used to say, "My picture is not going to sell anything! And besides, if people have to see a picture, we're in the wrong business." No one bought Milton to see Milton, to look at his picture.

L.P.   *That's very Jewish!*

J.H.   Ahahah!

L.P.   *It's very "Jewish" to think what is important is the book and not the photograph, that writing is an activity on its own, a sacred activity for the book, with white and black, paper and letters, but not for the person who's the writer.*

J.H.   Hmm . . . the anonymity of the Book. Written by God, the Author—but not in a literal, fundamentalist sense. "God" here means simply not written by any identifiable ego. What makes the book important, authoritative, is just that it had no author.

L.P.   *There are cultures that don't pay any attention to the identity of the writer or pay less attention to it because the writer is a writer within a tradition. So it's not the writer who speaks but a series of books, a tradition, that's speaking through the scribe. Then there are other cultures that stress very strongly the identity, the authority and the personality of the individual writer and shift the stress from the book itself to the set of values which is literally impersonated by the biographical symbol, the persona of the writer. . . .*

J.H.   If one can create a *persona* of the writer, if one can create a figure like Oscar Wilde or William Faulkner, how he created himself into being a character, or if one could create a figure the way J. P. Donleavy made himself into "the writer"—then you can tell your stories and the stories are all literary events at the same time; they're not biographical, they're fables. But since I can't do that, it seems the only other path is the anonymous path. It's like the difference between being Irish and Jewish. And that Irish-Jewish thing has been in my psyche since I was a boy. . . . It's a very American pattern; the Irish attracted to the Jews, the Jews attracted to the Irish: Norman Mailer has Irish characters in his books, Joyce puts the Jews in his book; peculiar symbiosis of the Irish and the Jews. . . .

L.P. *Joyce says that what the Irish and the Jews have in common is that they both speak a dead language. . . .*

J.H. Well, they have something else in common—they can't make it into the British world! There is a certain bourgeois correct Protestant mode neither the Irish nor the Jews quite fit, and in America that long symbiotic connection as comedians, as theater people; entertainment again. It breaks up Protestant literalism.

Now, there's another way one can tell one's story, which you would probably say is Jewish, too, which is as lesson, as a parable: "Oh, once I did so-and-so." And that can be told within a context in order to make a point. That's all. It isn't biography, it's simply a parable, part of teaching, and very often I can use some piece of my life that way: I can do that when practicing analysis or teaching it, but it is specific to a certain moment, working with somebody over something specific. It must be apt, exactly fitting into what you are working on and for the sake of that something else, so it isn't biography any longer. That's another use of biography, that's the parabolical, the rabbinical use.

L.P. *I still want to understand more about how you became an analyst.*

J.H. You could say it was a typical Jewish bourgeois collective phenomenon of the early 1950s: the sociological answer. You could say, I had had psychological abilities since adolescence and had already begun to be a therapist when I worked in the Navy hospital. You could say it was unresolved transference on my analyst. You could say that my symptoms were a shamanistic beginning, an initiation into psychic reality—the spiritual answer. How many more answers should we look for?

L.P. *Did Jung himself have anything to do with it?*

J.H. His writings became more and more important. I put myself completely in the mold. But it wasn't directly Jung. In fact, it's funny to say, but I didn't even try to see Jung, even when I could have. I saw him at lectures or parties in the fifties, and sometimes met with him about Institute matters, but there were four years when I had opportunities to go there and I never did.

L.P. *Why?*

J.H. A peculiar feeling of self-protection. I was shy, I was embarrassed, a kind of schizoid cut-offness despite how I seemed to be cocky and confident. I don't want to make too much of the shyness, but it has always been there and still is when I am with superior persons. I am even shy about myself. I mean, I have trouble with this autobiography because it makes every little thing in my life sound so important. This is a complex reaction, and it is also a resistance to being overwhelmed by importance, by the "superior person." Self-protection, as I said.

L.P. *Was Jung overwhelming?*

J.H. Yes, extraordinarily, he was a huge, physical man, with huge feet, and he was an overpowering man, and I suppose I had my tiny thoughts beginning, and I didn't want to feel overwhelmed, being burned by being too close to the sun.

L.P. *Did Jung burn many people?*

J.H. I don't know if he burned many people, but he certainly arranged their complexes to point in his direction—to change the metaphor: it was as if he was like a huge magnet so that your complex would go . . . the needle would point that way, and you might lose your own connection to the North because of the force in him. So, to many of my Jungian friends Jung appears dead or dying in their dreams as time goes on, as if Jung has to "die" in order for them to become whatever they are. The identification of the man with his ideas and with their "self" image has to come apart.

L.P. *Do you remember the first time you met him?*

J.H. The first time that I saw him, I just saw him; he came into the Psychological Club to listen to a lecture and he . . . it was the tremendous impressiveness of his stature . . . and everyone whispering that he was present. Like the chief of the tribe or the Holy

Man has come in. You see, Jung was sustained by an aura or a cult, at least at the end of his life when I saw him. That is a spiritual phenomenon, the transformation of psyche into spirit, and it is part of what has happened to Jungian psychology from being psychology to being a spiritual teaching, a path, a wisdom, a doctrine. It belongs to a certain time in history, too. We can't do that any more. We don't take ourselves or let ourselves be taken that importantly. There is too much debunking nowadays, too much irony. My God, when you see the photographs of the Great Men, say at early Eranos conferences, or at the Psychoanalytic Congresses, there is such a mystique! Maybe the interview and the talk show and the panel have their virtue after all, maybe they have helped knock off that spiritual crap about Greatness.

L.P. *But Jung was a great man, nevertheless, no matter how we define "greatness."*

J.H. Oh, yes, he was! And it was there when you saw him, or so it seemed. You see, it's so hard to know about these things. Remember the *Wizard of Oz?* Greatness has so much to do with expectations, too. So that even your own witness to what you saw becomes a question. I remember his wife's funeral in 1955. He walked into the church in the front from a side door with about nineteen members of his family, children, grandchildren, an enormous procession, the patriarch with his following, his great fertility, the old man and his tribe. That was an impressive, patriarchal, dominating figure. But I have other kinds of personal reminiscences.

Once we were out in his garden, and a little plane went over making a lot of noise and he observed, "Heavenly farts." He was probably doing what we call "an indirection," that is, he was bringing the conversation down, putting us back inside our shoes. Do you see how tales about Jung become like Zen stories? When I saw him in March before he died in June, he had a Zen book, or a Chinese master's book, on the table where we sat.

L.P. *What else do you remember of Jung?*

J.H. What I like to remember are things like his getting derailed over Albert Schweitzer. Someone must have set him off by asking a question about Schweitzer at one of our little discussions at his house, and Jung just couldn't stop . . . .

L.P. *What was it with Schweitzer?*

J.H. Oh, Jung couldn't abide the piousness, and Schweitzer's escape from the European predicament by retreating into the white man's colonial jungle where it is easy to do "good works." But that's not my point. Why I like to recall this little incident is that Jung had his peeves, his rages, and it came out over a rival senex figure. I mean it's instructive to see how one old wise man hates another old wise man, and that the hatred and showing it is exactly what distinguishes Jung from Schweitzer. It is great to see that when you are a student and trying to hide your shadow. It may have been in that same meeting that someone asked Jung about the shadow, and he said "It shows right here, in your face." But let's leave these Stories of the Master because really I knew Jung very, very peripherally, and these kinds of stories put me into a student-disciple-son kind of complex.

L.P. *When you were in India and before that in Dublin and Paris, you had been writing. Were you still writing when you went into analysis and began to study in Zurich?*

J.H. No, that was part of the trouble, I guess, now looking back. I wrote only in connection with the analysis—dreams, interpretations, dialogues with imaginal figures. I couldn't write anything else. You have to understand I was *completely* in the analysis. Maybe that was American, too, that naive devotion. But I don't regret that at all. That's the way you learn: enter a discipline. You have to feel it, your heart has to be in it. When your heart is really in it, then there is a chance to work your way through it. Otherwise you stay in a kind of eclectical half-doubt, and there's no real passion involved. It's eclectic, it's selective, comparing and choosing and criticizing—all ego. Because who does the selecting? The ego. I think ego-psychology results from this eclectic approach to learning rather than a passionate approach. You have to be a follower, a devotee of the heart to be saved from ego-psychology. You even have to suffer the embarrassment of your passion. So my soul was all in it, and I went with the Jungian thing totally, and then my soul began to leave it and I began to leave it—at least, as a disciple.

L.P.   *When did you begin to leave it?*

J.H.   That came much later. But first I was very Jungian. The Institute was everything to me, and I even signed up at the University of Zurich for the sake of the Institute. Now there's an image: I signed my name in the registry at the University of Zurich and broke into a tremendous sweat, the whole body, like I walked right into my fate and put my name down in the Big Book— which was only a university registry.

L.P.   *Why did you sign?*

J.H.   I had already an M.A. from Dublin, but that, that was the life of Evelyn Waugh, Brideshead Revisited, that was a beautiful mixture of literary, philosophy, society, English girls, Irish poets, fantasy, drinking, that was something else. It was beautiful. Beautiful. But Zurich, the University of Zurich, was grim, . . . and ancestral. My grandfather on my mother's side was born in eastern Germany, and I could hear all that seriousness coming back, and so my body broke into a sweat from the top of my head to my feet—ahhhhhgh. That was 1953 in November, and I did six years of the University and the Jung Institute. I had clinical patients, and I wrote a dissertation—that was my first book, *Emotion*—and I did everything properly. I came out of the University with a summa cum laude, even though I was an American and the whole thing was in German. I did it; but I never opened my mouth at that University, I sat in every seminar in silence. It was an initiation . . . going through the Underworld . . . it was unbelievable . . . I did not learn a thing. I don't know what I learned, honestly. In Dublin, which was all fun, I learned a lot.

L.P.   *It was erotic. You seemed to have had your anima there.*

J.H.   This ought to tell us something about studying . . . it just must never be given over to the academic senex. I went to lectures in Zurich by Buber and by Heidegger and by Ludwig Binswanger, I even heard Anna Freud—but not one goddam thing registered. Nothing. I can see Buber's white beard still and the way Heidegger wiggled his big backside and spoke with a high voice and how Binswanger looked like my own relatives (my maternal side is Binswanger way back, so we are blood cousins), but I didn't take anything in. I am not a good pupil. I never was a student of a master; I don't look back on any particular teachers or professors.

L.P. *And at the Jung Institute?*

J.H. Now that was different. I soaked it up. It probably was— objectively speaking, academically speaking—only third rate, many of the courses, most of the teachers, but, there was a madness there, a spirit, and I took in every word; I loved the material.

L.P. *What about your own cases that you saw in your training at the Institute?*

J.H. I had the usual control cases, and I remember that the Gods seemed to favor me with mainly older women, much older. One had been in a women's prison during the war; one came from a family of suicide after suicide—by hanging and cutting the throat; one was so awful that no one in her family ever spoke to her. I had those cases at first; there I was, Hans Castorp, "life's delicate child" right in the middle of rough older women, and that made me more shaky about the whole business than ever. So I had in my training some very long and difficult cases. I went to Burghölzli and sat in on the morning diagnostic sessions; I was given a key and could work with patients in the worst wards. Later on, I was teaching courses in therapy and giving exams and had trainees. Then ... well ... there came a moment when, in 1969–70–71, I stopped doing therapy, in fact I stopped completely for probably eighteen months. I had a physical reaction against doing it.

I thought nothing I had done from '55 to '69 was authentic, that everything I did I had learnt. It was like an illness, a physical illness, and when anybody mentioned patients, my whole body moved away from it ... and they'd say, "Look, you haven't seen anybody; don't you think you should keep yourself in it," and I just pulled away from it, like a horse. I didn't want anything to do with analysis. I wouldn't, I couldn't sit down in either chair. I felt I had only been doing what I had been taught, that it was all a fake, that it was all sentimental, that it was all personalistic in some way, that I had been doing things, manipulating, that I hadn't understood. I criticized myself completely, as if every bit of my analytical work had been wrong. Certain images from therapeutic sessions five years before, two years, seven years, would come back and I would be nauseated with myself or therapy. So that was a *crise de foi* and was extremely important. Extremely. I realized what oppression doing therapy had been, what a burden, how much guilt was involved, how I was carrying people, how I was trying to make them well, how I was ... oh, my goodness! Then I began again, slowly, ... of course, the judgments about what I had been doing were part of this internal revolution. I can't say that I was right, that I had been doing bad therapy or good therapy, that isn't the point. The point is in the emotion I had about it all and the resistance, the doubt. Looking back, I can see that the breakdown of my doing therapy took place at the same time as my first marriage was untying and the re-visioning book on therapy was forming.

L.P. *When you began again how was it different from previous therapy*?

J.H. Looking back, it seems another model was forming. I found a new fantasy of it. You know what it was? It was the coming together of, well, of my *biography*—hah! I imagined myself working in my room, like having a sculpture studio, and anybody who wanted to work with me in the studio could come and make iron sculptures with me. Fine, I'll show you how I do it, let's do it together, let's work on this; welding iron. It wasn't any longer "I'm curing your psyche," "I'm your analyst," or even "I interpret or counsel" or anything to do with therapy. Therapy was contained now in another fantasy *outside* of therapy, let's call it the "art fantasy," so that therapy was no longer literal. We're two people working together on psychic material, and that material is not our feelings, our transference, back and forth, because to identify psychic material with subjective feelings, no matter how intense, is just bad art. And bad therapy, too, I was beginning to see. In other words I was finding a way of doing therapy with an artist's fantasy which didn't literalize either art or therapy—or the patient—and which allowed in even more feelings because they weren't so sticky, so overvalued. So the model of being a therapist, of carrying another soul only as far as I had come myself—one of Jung's cautions—of guiding, of successful or failed cases—all those models which burdened me . . .

L.P. *And now?*

J.H. Now it is just taking the material that comes and working with it, and I love that. It doesn't matter whether it is people's lives or their dreams or their symptoms or their feelings—it's all psychological material, scrap iron for sculpting. The responsibility question dropped away, judging myself and pushing myself dropped away. It doesn't mean I don't feel anxious and concerned and upset when things go wrong or when people I'm working with get into a mess or nothing seems to happen. Of course, you get tired, and there are bad hours, bad periods—like anywhere else. Of course, you get caught by what goes on; but the caughtness itself is different. It's enjoyable, somehow. Let's say the sculpture is doing more of the sculpting than I am. The psyche is making itself. It's a shift to soul-making as I called it, working and shaping psychological stuff.

L.P. *You seem to have always been questioning therapy.* Suicide and the Soul *and the essays in* The Myth of Analysis, *also written in the sixties, raise fundamental questions about the nature of psychotherapy. You begin the essay on Eros by asking what "fathers" psychotherapy, what is its generating principle and its basic myth.*

J.H. That's true. In fact one of my angers about my colleagues is that they seem so smug in what they do. They don't seem to question the act of therapy itself. Or, if they do raise questions, they end up with sentimental statements of belief, trust in "the process," in God's kind hands or instinct or whatever. But still, this breakdown in 1969–70–71—that was more than just questioning. It was in my body: I couldn't go on doing it. I was too ashamed. My body couldn't do it.

L.P. *"Your body couldn't do it"—that seems to be a determining factor like how you have mentioned your illnesses, your fears. And yet, in your writings there is not much space given to body.*

You write much more about fantasies, mythic images, feelings, and you seem to locate psyche with reflection.

J.H.   Don't you think writing is a kind of therapeutic act to fill up the holes? I mean, don't you think we urge ourselves in our writings, like they are sermons to ourselves or ways of fulfilling wishes? I write about all sorts of things—like reflection—I don't necessarily *do*, but might wish I could do or think I should do. The writing is a way of doing those things. In actual fact, body determines a great deal of my life in every sort of way. And the readers of the books, the pupils—they don't know that at all. They miss the animal. The whole work is based on the animal. So the books are deceptive.

L.P.   *Then maybe the interview does have a valuable purpose: it can correct too-intellectual, reflective, fantasyful notions about you and your work.*

J.H.   To give a reader a "true" picture? Hmmm. But don't you think that anybody who reads the books or goes to a lecture—supposedly such an intellectual thing—would pick up at once that there is an animal around. The energy, the style, the flow, the leaps and flights—I mean . . .

L.P.   *. . . you mean, not to read you literally, but to pick up the tone.*

J.H.   Yes and I mean also that reflection and intellect and fantasy aren't opposite to body but go with it and come out of it. Let's not get caught in some opposition between body and fantasy.

L.P.   *Your "Essay on Pan" is precisely on that relation. It shows how fantasy is always going on in behavior and behavior is always a kind of fantasy.*

J.H.   You see, as we talk now, these words we say back and forth, where do they come from? They aren't reflected: they just come out, the way a monkey swings on a branch or a sheep ambles over to try a little bit of grass over there. The whole thing starts with the animal. And that is the instructive purpose of what I would like to get over, what I intend with talking about myself. It's not the biography: what I did, where I was, what I felt, and so

on. It's the way one trusts the animal that carries the whole thing
forward, including this interview. You didn't, I didn't, expect to
be talking about the animal vehicle as they call it in India, but
here it is—it came in, and nothing could be more important to
how I feel about myself, than this animal.

L.P.   *And animals don't have biographies.*

J.H.   No, they don't have to tell stories. They just show themselves. They are like images. They *are* images.

L.P.   *Therefore your reason for not being biographical—what
you said earlier—that you can't make images of your life and that
you prefer just to do your work, is because you want to show, to
be, that animal?*

J.H.   Let's go at it this way. These questions about my life in the
Navy or in Zurich: are they really about my life? Aren't they
really trying to get at something more than biography, something
more than the history of events or the revelation of character?
Aren't they trying to get some lore, to break into myth? What
makes a figure is the lore. Take the Beat Generation, Kerouac;
their lore made them more than they were. We can't get rid of
Nixon, no way to forget him, just because of the lore. Then look
at Gerald Ford—absolutely loreless. Freud and Jung are full of
lore, and it still goes on; so they are still very much alive as figures in the imagination. We keep on learning from them,
through the lore. I often think training into a school means learning its lore. Gossip is vital to the educative process: it's how you
pick up the *Lebensphilosophie*, how you learn how that tradition
handles life. But lore makes you—if you're the one gossiped
about—into a kind of mythical figure. It may be good for the
tradition, but what does it do to you? So we have to ask again:
Why do we need biographies at all? Who wants them—what part
of us needs biographies? We need images, figures, like tribal stories of heroes and legends so that we can live our lives more . . .
with more vision, more inspiration. So we can survive. So this
biography isn't about me, sitting here with you, in an armchair.
It's about the figure "James Hillman"—and who is that, who is
he? He is an image, and so this interview is engaged in creating

or adding to or polishing that image. We are desperate for these images, they are foundational . . . but it's not the me sitting here, it's James Hillman, author, who then through the interview becomes an authority.

L.P. *A foundational image seems to settle upon a human person, and so that human person becomes a founder, a founding father and a founder of a school or a movement, like archetypal psychology. And around the foundational image various legends form and hero cults.*

J.H. And also death wishes and hatreds! There is a paranoid part to this, too, you know, as well as an inflating part. But it's not me who does this. It's the nature of the founding image that calls for embellishments, emotions; image has a kind of life of its own and that is what biography ultimately serves; that's the archetypal, the mythical purpose. Oh, sure, biography has social history and personal complexes in it and so on, but that's not what makes biography important for survival. It's the presence of the foundational image—this figure presenting itself, displaying itself—like an animal, to go back to where we were. It's like being a living totem pole, so there is death in it, too.

L.P. *Is there no relation at all between the "you" sitting in the armchair, talking now, and the mythical James Hillman? Surely that is precisely what biography is about: that relationship.*

J.H. That question is a whole lifetime. It has to do with who one is ultimately. I have no idea. All I can say is that this interview, this biography, puts me into the service of a James Hillman. This "I" feels obliged to sit here each afternoon all week long because somebody wants a book. And this James Hillman can become a monster and eat up my life, and that's why I don't want pictures on my books and why I am sloppy in shaving and why I have trouble with TV and interviews. I'm afraid of the effect of lore. I have to admit I want to control my life and not let it be taken over by story. Becoming even the least bit mythical is no joke; it makes for heroes, and then you are doomed. I'm afraid of archetypal psychology paying me back in kind—myth—and turning me into something it needs. The "me" is protecting himself against this goddam James Hillman. I don't know how to carry this founding image gracefully. . . .

L.P. *Nevertheless, it must be carried. Founding images are necessary to a culture. They help sustain its spirit. Besides, if these founding figures are like the culture's animal totems, then don't you have some sort of social, or cultural responsibility toward the figure "James Hillman"? Your service to it goes beyond your own personal interests. Didn't Jung write about this question in his discussion of the mana-personality, that the mana-personality fulfills the mana need of the culture?*

J.H. I don't feel myself a mana carrier. I don't have any special—what shall I say—mysticality. I'm just jammed full of ordinary things, boring things. I play baseball. I cook meals. I like to go to the supermarket. I read the newspapers. I call my mother on the phone. I call my brother. Does a mana carrier, does a founding image call his mother on the phone? After all, I was born in Atlantic City which is all show and sham and shabby deals and auction houses and fake importance. We grew up "seeing through"! Mana there means fake, flashy. That's why I obsessively refer to the work, the books, and why the activity of writing itself is where you might catch a glimpse of mana, or I like better to say, the animal in action. I ought to correct that: when I say writing, I really mean other things too, like lecturing, like practicing analysis. It's wherever the animal is acting fully in its image. Where imagination is going on. Yes, we need these images of founding figures. The figure configurates or exemplifies the archetypal activity of writing or teaching or healing. The figure allows these activities to go on, but it isn't the person. You see, it's not the me inside James Hillman, and it's not even James Hillman; it's the archetypal figure of teacher or whatever that allows teaching or whatever to go on. We have to have figures, and I guess we have to have biographies, just so the culture can go on.

7 OLD AND NEW— SENEX AND PUER

L.P. *In reading all you have written one hardly ever finds references to what is modern: you hardly ever report on your cases, and in speaking of culture, your models come always from the old humanistic classical culture. The old culture has the upper hand. Why?*

J.H. The old culture has the upper hand because I think it's more important! One reason—you are looking for reasons—is that living in America I see the danger of connecting everything to what is immediately topical. America is a complete immersion in what is happening; it's a Now-culture, utterly Now. So, involvement with the past should be seen as a way of stepping out of the Now, rather than making social comments on it. Of course, that step is already a comment because you can't really step out of where you are. There is nowhere else to step to. The Renaissance is not another place or another time. It's a mode of being in Now or looking at Now and talking about it. But it means that my comment doesn't have to be stated in Now language. The very fact that I talk in mythical and historical terms is my comment on Now. Those are fantasy landscapes by means of which you can see the Now or save the phenomenon from being lost in Now.

L.P. *So the reason you moved to the Renaissance in your latest books . . .*

J.H. . . . It's evident that in a culture that is floating and lost I'm making the same move that people made at other times; they went back. In the Renaissance—and they were lost then, too— they went back. This is a move made by artists, by thinkers, by cultures, the move of going back so that one stands somewhere. . . .

L.P.   *More solid? The past better than the present?*

J.H.   No, not solid: but one has an eye that has been trained by stepping back. . . .

L.P.   *The eye of the old?*

J.H.   Yes, the old eye, the call of the old, and it may be the essential eye. It is to gain essence, not time: it's to train the eye to read and the hand to make the right move and not simply because it's old. I think that calling it "old" is already a prejudice of the Now. The Now is not a matter of time. The Now is simply the unreflected, the naturalistic perspective, the way things happen, the "forgetful" as the phenomenologists say. "Now" means here, close, appearance; therefore distance, depth, and essence are given by the old. Now-consciousness doesn't understand that the old has nothing to do with time. The old doesn't belong to the senex in some sterile dusty way. If you see the Renaissance as old, you are in Now-consciousness. I don't see the Renaissance as old, I see the Renaissance as having been concerned with the same things, but more essentially. I don't see tradition as historical, I see tradition as contemporary, as informing what we do, what we feel. What is it that still makes people so interested in Greek temples, pyramids, Riace's bronzes or Altamira caves? It is not history: that's only the first level of it, people asking themselves, "Oh, my goodness, people did this four thousand years ago, isn't that extraordinary, they could build these pyramids without modern cranes?" That's the first level of the reaction. But after that first impact, which begins to break down the Now, the level and the quality change and one gets in touch with something essential. Essential doesn't necessarily mean that it has to have been there for a thousand years. But in some way, being in a Greek temple or seeing the pyramids or seeing the graffiti on the walls of a cave in Spain evokes the eternal, essential images of the soul. It does not have to be the actual pyramid that I am seeing: that is the literalism of it. You are seeing the ancient images, the archetypal images, not merely the pyramids themselves: but seeing the pyramids evokes the archetypal sense that there are eternal images, and those give you a sense of essence.

L.P.   *What do you mean exactly by eternal images, archetypal images?*

J.H.   What makes us able to be in touch with what we are given, the forms of recognitions, the basis my knowledge is founded on, everything that I sense of being right or being off, doing it right or wrong, the governing bodies of my imagination—those are the essential images. And they are essentially human; they are what make me human and deepen my compassion for human history, let me understand things, feel into things way beyond the limits of my personal education and personal experience. You see, by opening up the essential imagination we also expand our compassion.

L.P.   *That is the old argument of the humanists, too: the belief that culture expands the heart and makes it more sensitive, 'human.'*

J.H.   It's how I understand "morality," too. If you don't have those governing bodies of imagination, if you don't have an eternal, archetypal sense in the midst of the Now, then you don't have any sense of where you are going, what structure you are in, and your animal response is off. Instinct. Jung said that instinct and images are the same thing. When you lose that sense of the essential images, then instinct is off and you build ugly buildings, and you overeat, you become obese, and your whole structure is disoriented. You become immoral. I mean irrelevant, without any instinct, sort of anesthetized. I go back more and more to old places, not because that is where essence *is,* but because it evokes the *sense* of essence. So I definitely do not mean that you "have to know history": it's not history, but a sense of essence, and that deliteralizes history. That is very important because history is such a big burden when it's taken as a senex thing. . . .

L.P.   *It kills everything.* . . .

J.H.   It kills everything, absolutely. History is nothing at all in itself—just a statue in the park for pigeons. Only as an avenue for seeing the Now in perspective is it valuable. You can't see up close; everything flattens out. You don't have to *make* history relevant, because once you have a historical sense then it gives relevance and sorts out the trivia in events by giving perspective.

L.P. *"Perspective" appears again and again in your writings. You speak of the Gods as perspectives and that myths give us perspectives, so that we can see events differently. Could you say more about your notion of "perspective"?*

J.H. I'd like to come at it in terms of something I've been thinking about recently. Old and new, or what we've been calling essential and Now, can be seen in terms of foreground and background in Gestalt psychology. Whatever you focus on becomes a foreground, that is, really *seen,* if there is a background. Take any event that's obsessing us, some item of Now—some symptom, some topic in the news, some argument in psychology like narcissism—it's just utterly, immediately up-close and literal. But the moment we bring in the Renaissance or Egypt or Greek myth, the moment we introduce a phrase from Shakespeare or Keats, we see it as a foreground phenomenon. It's tied into a background; it can resonate. It's still up-close and blown up, but it has become suddenly relativized; because it has background, it is *only* foreground. The Now becomes only now and not the whole Gestalt. It becomes an image and not just an event. It's the same way with cases. They are only cases, utterly literal real people with real problems until we get an essential perspective, some kind of background, an archetypal fantasy, if you like. Then the cases become images. But be careful here, not images *of* the archetypal myths or fantasies—that's to get into a Platonic argument—but images as foreground phenomena because there is a background. History is one way of making a gestalt: historical references, figures from the past release the foreground event from being stuck in only what it says it is.

L.P. *But this is also a rhetorical topos, the past as a "topos" that makes sublime everything that is being talked about, whereas the present is used as a way of trivializing the argument. . . .*

J.H. That's of course senex—the perspective of Saturn, the old established wisdoms: the past deepens, makes more valid, becomes proof. You know, this is a classical, Latin way of proving something: "Truth stands the test of time." But if one is at the opposite pole of this senex mode of consciousness, if one is in the archetype of the child, if a puer, youthful myth is dominating, as is often the case when you are fourteen and even when you are much older, then you throw out every reference to the past as out of the question. History and time would ruin your position completely. The puer never learns with time and repetition: he resists development and is always unique. No precedents, no past—that's how it feels to him. A culture in that archetype, like our culture, cannot help but be radically against the past, against what has already become and therefore is not unique. This shows in every aspect of the culture. For example, an American textbook in sociology, psychology, anthropology, even history, cannot be more than three years old or it will not be listed in the catalogs . . . three years old and the book has to be revised. Instant revision! Only the newest is valid.

L.P. *When you introduced the idea of "re-visioning" you didn't mean "up-dating" or modernizing. You meant rather looking again, gaining a new vision based on going back. Is your book* Re-visioning Psychology *a new psychology or an old one?*

J.H. Why ask that question? What difference does it make? It keeps us paralyzed in the puer-senex: new or old. The main thing is to recognize that the really new is not the Now. It's more like re-new. What matters is the little syllable "re"—that's the most important syllable in psychology: remember, return, revision, reflect . . .

L.P. *. . . recognition, which is a knowledge coming from what is already in the soul and in the culture.*

J.H. Yes, and response. Responding to what's right there.

L.P. *React . . .*

J.H. Yes, re-act, both as repeating and responding . . .

J.H. *Repetition would be a way of "going back."*

J.H. These are the important words—even repent and remorse—religious words.

L.P. *Re-ligion itself has been explained to mean linking or tying back . . .*

J.H. . . . or connecting again. Of all these "re" words, maybe the most important is re-spect, which means to look again. Did you

know that? And that's all that psychology does, that's the whole
thing in a single word. That's what our dreams are doing and our
memories: bringing us to respect ourselves—not *in*spect with
guilt—to re-gard what happened yesterday, what happened in
childhood and re-spect it. We look again at what was forgotten or
repressed, we even look again at the mechanisms of forgetting
and repressing, and whatever we look at again we gain a new
respect for—whether in ourselves or the culture. But to do this,
you have to let it be as it is and not try to up-date it, make it new.
Just the looking again, the respect, renews it. The up-dating process is constantly wiping out history; nothing in our culture is
more hated, more repressed than the old. There is a desperate
fear of the senex, as if he were Old George the Third—senex
turned into ogre. But the senex is also the old wise man, the old
whale, the old ape. And if you stick only with the new and the
future, you only have the bluebird or the mosquito: no whale, no
old ape. We still are all positivists; we believe you move forward
by turning against the past, whereas in the Renaissance we move
forward by looking backward—that was a favorite maxim. So was
Philosophia duce regredimur. . . .

L.P.   *Aren't you now doing exactly what I said a moment ago:
using the rhetorical topos of the past, or let's say, the senex, in
order to ennoble the old?*

J.H.   Oh, sure! The puer could come along and say: historical references to the Renaissance deaden an argument while references
to *Star Wars* make it lively, relevant, immediate. This teaches us
that we are always in one or another archetypal style of rhetoric.
You can't open your mouth without an archetypal perspective
speaking through you. Rhetoric doesn't mean just the art or system of persuasive argument; by rhetoric I mean that all speech is
rhetorical in that every archetype has its own mode of rhetoric,
its way of persuading you.

L.P.   *Again, the Renaissance, especially the Italian Renaissance.
. . . Why?*

J.H.   I do not talk of the Renaissance as a "philologue" or as anyone knowledgeable about the culture. . . . I don't regard myself in
any way to be a scholar of Greece or of the Renaissance or of

history. I don't see myself as an historian, but I feel that these materials are our roots, our Western historical roots, and they have been locked up by the academics, put into universities, put into museums, so we citizens, you and I, have been cut off from our roots by the academics who claim they are educating people to have culture, but who actually cut us off from culture because they've made it a preserve of the academic. You have to go through decades of scholarly brainwashing in order to work on the Renaissance. It needs to be opened up again for the citizen to reclaim his own culture. . . . We live in a terrible split. Maybe the Renaissance did, too, but they had maxims for healing the split, like *gloria duplex,* keeping the consciousness of both sides. The danger lies in splitting the duplex into only senex or only puer. Exclusive. One turned against the other. We had one-sided puer in the sixties, and now that chaotic style of destruction is giving way to a programmed style of senex destruction—political repression, armaments, CIA again—in the name of economics and security, which are senex ideals. If *gloria duplex* sounds too old-fashioned, too Italian for you, then what about our little syllable "re"? It takes the old and gives it a puer twist. It turns things back and turns things upside down at the same moment.

L.P. *How else can you imagine the re-union of senex and puer?*

J.H. I think first we have to watch out for anything simple. Simplifications are already part of the rhetoric of one or another side of the split. *Gloria duplex* means complicated answers, not many single answers lined up as alternative scenarios. A string of alternatives is not what I mean by "poly" which is always complex. The Renaissance, as Edgar Wind depicts it, for instance, spoke of *complicatio* instead of *explanatio* or *simplicitas*. When we complicate in the right way we begin to force imagination to work. Simplification stops the imagination . . . as we imagine the world, as we imagine our historical problems, they begin to be interiorized, they begin to be psychological. But it isn't we who make those complications—it's the psyche, the anima. That's what anima does—messes things up, blurs the edges. She gets things tangled—isn't that what "plicated" means, folded? So the beginning of a puer-senex reunion means letting the anima get at both sides, letting the dried-out senex feel soul again, little bits of moisture, little gipsy fantasies, and letting the high-flying, fire-eating puer feel inferior and moody and confused. A little lonely and outcast and misunderstood like the senex. It's so hard to realize that big pathological problems can have fuzzy solutions, pathological solutions. The only difference between the dangerous old admiral and the wise old whale is that anima connection.

L.P. *Then there is a great difference between your devotion to the old as a mode of giving value and essence and simply being caught in the senex as a conservative or a patriarch—tradition glorified for its own sake and used to suppress the young.*

J.H. The main task for me is to keep in touch with the senex in all its different facets. The senex slips in unawares—not just in depressions and cruelties. It's very easy to become unconscious of the senex as a *psychological* factor because it tends to concretize its perspective as "real," "hard," and "out there" . . . economics, for instance . . . Saturn as fixations into literalisms and materialized abstractions.

L.P. *This seems to be again a lack of concern for the concrete world and its laws, so common with the Jungians. . . .*

J.H. Isn't that the senex speaking right there in your sentence? I'm not at all unconcerned with the concrete world, the world of matter, just the contrary! I'm writing on all sorts of material questions, even chemistry and bus transportation and downtown buildings. But one particular *view* of matter—call it scientific, economic, sociological—is killing our civilization slowly. Or it will kill it fast by setting up the puer in his exclusive one-sidedness . . . then the puer will react and kill the worldview of the senex quickly, anarchically, the fire of apocalypse. So the job of psychology is to keep senex always in some sort of psychological context, to keep Saturn from becoming paranoid, antisocial, which is potential in his nature. That's why I struggle so with monotheism: I see Saturn in it, his dangerous "singleness of vision." That senex intolerance and blindness could wipe us all out. By blindness I mean particularly soulless concreteness.

L.P. *Your approach to the material world—even if it is concrete, is not soulless. Isn't that what you mean when you call for con-*

*crete immediacy, for instinct and instinctual attention to the actu-
al material world?*

J.H. Exactly! My approach to the world is via the *anima mundi,*
as a world *ensouled*. The senex, as we have been talking of it just
now, is fixated *literally* on the concrete—economics, power politics, energy, whatever—without any psychological, without any
anima overtone. The world for the senex, as we have been speaking of it, is not an expression of soul; it is the countervalence of
soul. And this soulless concretism dominates both the N-bomb
project and the terroristic attitude, and this shows that they share
the same archetypal reality, the same insanity. Both think what is
most real are the physical and external structures. Soulless concretism. I think what's most real are the structures of consciousness, of imagination, so that when ideas move, when the mind
moves, when the images move, then the other things also move.
By attacking and defending the same concrete and institutional
structures both sides reinforce the very conflict. The Old Guard
and the Red Guards only make each other stronger and don't
conserve anything or renew anything. The soul isn't really
touched so nothing moves. The anarchic, the terrorist vision is to
my mind very old-fashioned, an early-nineteenth-century vision
of reality that we have to see through and let go of—prepsycholo-
gical, premetaphorical, prephenomenological. On the other hand
psychoanalysis needs more dissidents, more even than Laing and
the antipsychiatric movement; it needs its own "terrorists of
soul" in the sense of a radical seeing through of its fixed invest-
ments in profession—its banks and insurance, its law courts, its
palaces of bureaucracy—to return soul to the world.

L.P. *This sounds messianic, like the rhetoric of the puer again.*

J.H. Why not—for a moment at least! Doesn't that just show
how the puer breaks through when one fantasies on the old. The
archetype of old and new can't really be separated. It seems better
to me to focus carefully, painfully on the old and let the puer
break in spontaneously as it just did now to us, rather than to
focus on the new so literally that the senex absorbs it and makes
it concrete and soulless in the same old dried-out patterns.

L.P. *This topic of old and new, of age and youth, is so very old itself, such a basic topos in literature, and it repeats in psychoanalysis in Oedipus and in Totem and Taboo, the fathers versus the sons; and yet it is always new. Expressing it with Latin terms deliberately keeps it old, and in our culture gives it a new sound. We can hear or see the questions differently. Conflicts of generations, renewal of civilization, conservatism versus radicalism— even arguments about style in art, architecture, and literature— can be conceived within this archetypal pair and thought about so as to enlighten conflict, making it more psychological, rather than merely to go on in the same old ways that are always presented as new ways.*

J.H. Enlightening conflicts means nothing more than making them psychological, remembering that the two, senex and puer, have to appear together. You can't have one without the other somewhere near.

L.P. *The terms themselves, senex and puer, illustrate so very well just what we have been talking about: the value of going back to the Italian Renaissance, which at the same time brings something fresh into psychology.*

8 ACROSS THE RIVER AND INTO THE STREET

L.P. *We were talking of continuity, tradition, and culture as essential to psychology. In this way you set the problem of psychology in time. How does time alter the conditions of psychoanalysis, of therapy?*

J.H. In my own life therapy was extremely important; probably because I submitted to therapy, years of analysis, that I became, I suppose, a psychologist, that it was felt in my own flesh, the sense of being pathological. I am not sure it is the same way in the 1980s. I wonder whether consciousness has not made a move so that the pathologizing in oneself, one's sense of one's shadow, isn't more built in without having to go into therapy. Before 1910–14, therapy wasn't crucial. They became analysts without long heavy analyses. It was the shift of consciousness that counted, joining the perspective of the Freudian vision.

L.P. *Analysis may be needed by each generation for different reasons. We can't always see the reasons. They are unconscious. But there is always an unconsciousness in each generation and that unconsciousness is the "reason" for analysis, today too.*

J.H. I'm trying to imagine that there has been a new shift of consciousness so that—through breakdown—the extensive endless therapy that was basic to the training of Freudians and Jungians earlier and in my day is no longer the same. People who have been five years in analysis today are not necessarily more psychologically acute than some people who have not been in analysis. Now that's a helluva thing to say, but I have to admit it. Is it because the ordinary person today is more psychologically acute, or is it because therapy is backward and dumb, still doing old tricks so that it doesn't sharpen people; it stultifies them? (I sure do sound antianalytical, don't I?)

L.P. *You said earlier that you enjoy doing analysis, yet you continue to talk against it. Can't you feel that others might enjoy it as you do?*

J.H. Or, sure—*enjoy* it; but don't pretend it's so useful in the old way, and don't demand it for everybody. As you say, unconsciousness is different and so analysis is no longer so useful for centering and introversion and self-actualization—all that subjectivism that was so crucial earlier. That's available in every deep-breathing workshop. So is dream work. So is body work. So is discovering the "inner feminine." The repressed is no longer like it was, no longer where it was.

L.P. *What is repressed today? Where is it today?*

J.H. It is hiding out there in public; disguised, like the devil always is, dressed in plain clothes, in the street. In Freud's time we felt oppressed in the family, in sexual situations, in our crazy hysterical conversion symptoms, and where we felt oppressed, there was the repressed. Where do we feel that thick kind of oppression today? In institutions—hospitals, universities, businesses; in public buildings, in filling out forms, in traffic....

L.P. *And personal relationships?*

J.H. Well . . . do we, really? Don't we know more about them—how to fight, how to make love, how to get out and start over. We are very psychological about the personal side of life now. The personal, the interior dimension is common public knowledge now. It's in the movies. There are so many films done by people who had no analysis that are extraordinarily acute psychologically, where I can learn all kinds of psychological things. There are students, kids, I learn from who have acuity that I don't have, even after years and years of psychology. The *Zeitgeist* is different. My generation had to endure intensive therapy to get out of the woods, to break the naturalistic ego we had, which was prephenomenological, premetaphorical, still caught in the narrative structures of the nineteenth century.

L.P. *How do these nineteenth-century narrative modes affect psychotherapy?*

J.H.   You know: a life story from beginning to end with a central figure, *me*. That's all broken up now. The hero's gone under the hill.

L.P.   *How are your students more acute than you believe you and your generation were?*

J.H.   For one thing, they are more connected—whatever that means. The society has spent thirty years discovering feeling and touching, and so they are more easy with feeling and touching. They are more aware about family influences—we were just *in* those influences. After all, psychoanalysis had to have yielded some awareness after all these years. The songs are different— with better metaphors and images. Drugs. They move more easily into different levels of consciousness. In fact, they don't even use that model of "levels of consciousness"; it's different psychic spaces, different places, many places. The very notion of the psyche has changed: more opened, more polytheistic. . . . Oh, I'm not an expert on postmodern consciousness. . . .

L.P.   *No shadow to it?*

J.H.   One mammoth one, just immense, and everywhere! Psychopathy. We aren't any longer in an age of anxiety or hysteria or even schizophrenia. I wish it were an age of depression and I work at that. No, as Adolf Guggenbühl says, It's all invisible psychopathy today. Very successful and very adapted and you can't see it. . . . People just do it, whatever it is. Now I live in Texas. People don't worry there, people don't have Viennese Jewish inhibitions, people don't come apart into schizophrenic *Zerfahrenheit:* they just do it in the world and make money, too. Shoot your father, shoot your son, rape, drink—the whole family drinks—drive the car and drink, take this drug or that, buy, buy, buy, change your face, lift your breasts, buy some hair, different hair for different occasions. Put in a new heart. Bypass the heart— what a metaphor! If you get tired of something, move out or sell or go bankrupt. Divorce it. If you want it, marry it. Transvestites, transsexuals, trans-you-name-it. I will name it: transcendence. There is something religious underneath that makes them transcend all their conditions. And this upward push pays off in economic success.

L.P. *You sound horrified.*

J.H. Well, I am, because there is no narcissism in this, no self-reflection, and no memory. No memory. They don't stay in the valley. People say about Texas that there are no real mountains, all flat. But Texans do have their immense big sky. What's really missing are the valleys, like in Switzerland, or the dark Viennese streets. Soul country. Depression. Closed in with one's demons. You know, when they use the word "development" in Dallas, they mean property, you know, land-development. They don't mean what New York and California mean: psychological, Jungian, internal development. At the same time it's all church-backed. Fundamentalist. Do you see what I am driving at? Psychopathic behavior is a fundamentalist behavior: taking fantasies literally and also confusing the literal and the concrete. Now this is just what the Fundamentalist churches support: if your arm offend thee, cut it off. If your nose offend thee, get it straightened. Looking at a woman with lust is the same as doing it; doing it in the psyche and doing it in the street become identical. If they say "tuck in your belly," they go out and take a tuck in it, surgically. If you need a lift, you get a face-lift. The metaphors become utterly concrete. It's all premodern consciousness—or its psychotic concretism! Exterior determines interior. When they discuss a new building in Dallas—and they are going up higher and faster and more than anywhere in America—they discuss the outside of it, how it looks, what's it covered with, as if no one would ever go inside these buildings. Life from a car window. I think they look at themselves that way, too. Inside is either terror of moral depravity or a kind of Muzak blankness, out of which pop moments of sentiment or some new idea for making money. But this concentration on the exterior is as I said economically rewarding.

L.P. *Texas might be a special case, and your view of it even more special.*

J.H. How about the world's fascination with Texas? Doesn't that show a world turning Texan, psychopathic in a similar way? The terrifying corporation mind, economics replacing value—as my friend there Robert Sardello says, cost-efficiency means the most return on the least investment: well, that's psychopathic, a moral deficiency and getting away with it. What's lost is interiorization, sensitivity, and real animal desires.

L.P. *Yet you live there. Why?*

J.H. Why? I never know "why" about anything. Why? is a bad question.

L.P. *Why?*

J.H. Hah. Good! Why because—hah, hah—because I like it there. See, now that's a psychopathic answer: do what you like, whatever you like, to whomever you like. No—we've good friends there and it's very good working there. Dallas is open in ways that are shut tight in Zurich. Of course, sitting here in Europe it's hard to see the virtue in this kind of city; of course, it looks psychopathic. But there is a slowness there, and a warmth—for instance, we live in a black section, old-fashioned, with wonderful talk. Everything happens on the porches, out in the street: phoning, music, visiting, shouting. Plenty of depression, too. And there is courtesy there and that way of joking and that way of walking in the heat. I get all kinds of images from my neighbors, all kinds of feelings. You know it was from the blacks that we got the word "soul" back into our language. So there's a good reason I like living in Dallas, but the real question isn't why, it's, *who* likes it in Dallas?

L.P. *Well, then, who?*

J.H. The missionary likes it because it is a desert there—aside from what I just said about the blacks across our street—it's a barren empty-souled place, so you can feel like Las Casas crossing Northern Mexico. And this cultural desert stimulates the missionary in me, or is it the alien, who likes being in impossible places. After all Zurich was an impossible place for a boy from Atlantic City: all the Swiss rocks and roots. Atlantic City doesn't have one single tree naturally. It's a sandbar, where I was born. The whole place is an *opus contra naturam*.

L.P. *Who else likes living in Dallas?*

J.H. The psychologist. I liked Zurich because it was so intensely psychological—everyone was. In Dallas it's the reverse—let's say, no one is . . . in that neurotic interior way; of course they are psychological in other ways, like business and politics. These extreme places, Zurich and Dallas, offer lots to the psychologist: Dallas is *the* modern city, *the* cultural challenge for psychology. You know Dallas is a fashion center. The syndromes appear just like fashions, they are worn right out in the street, this psychopathy and cultural vacuum and Christian fundmentalism or fanaticism, and this worship of economics, and grooming and spending a fortune on the physical body, the exterior body, and also the technological mind. A perfect example is jogging in the streets with earphones on your head—the body adapted to an electronic mind, no longer an animal or even a hunter of animals, but a very fine, a very expensive piece of equipment. You have to imagine Dallas like Vienna a hundred years ago, where neurosis and hysteria and sexual fantasies and family repression appeared all over the place. So Dallas is the ideal place to be immersed in the syndrome of one's time which I am calling psychopathy or psychotic concretism. This comparing Dallas with Vienna, this idea of cultural challenge means the culture-hero is talking now: he is the "who." You can see how Dallas gives the ideas I am working on a real soil in syndromes. Maybe there will be a Dallas School, just as the Zurich School came out of schizophrenia and the Vienna School came out of hysteria.

L.P. *I want to stay with your mode of answering the question— about "why" and "who" because it is a basic move in your* Re-Visioning Psychology. *You write:* "Why *takes one toward explanations or purposes . . .* who *dissolves the identification with one of the many insistent voices that fill us with ideas and feelings . . . in the last instance, the* who *refers to an archetypal figure."* You presented several who's *with which you can become identified: the culture-hero, the alien, the missionary, the psychologist, and so you would say these* who's *are the reason you are in Dallas.*

J.H. I would say these *who's* . . . and there are probably some others too . . . give me *reasons* why I am in Dallas. But if you pursue the *why* question instead of the *who*, it leads away from right here. *Why* leads into time. It leads into before and after, causes—"that's why I moved to Dallas, *because*." Or it leads to reasons, purposes, *telos*: I moved "in order to." It keeps you talking narratively, and answering from the "I": "*I* moved because *I*. . . ." It becomes introspective. It becomes moral, a justification to defend why I moved to Dallas. *Who*, on the other hand, is a fantasy answer. It opens into fantasy. It lets the little people in to have their say. The culture-hero, the alien, the fantasy of the missionary. It splits up the "I," or simply ignores the "I" by giving many different answers, some of which surprise the "I" very much. It makes the answer richer and more psychological because there is some self-reflection in it about the different perspectives that play through my mind and the move to Dallas. It's a move from monotheism to polytheism—not the move to Dallas! My goodness, not *that* move—the move from *why* to *who*.

L.P. *What you just said now, what you just did with me, and with the question of* why *seems to be teaching.*

J.H. Teaching, but not "a teaching." There was no content—I mean I didn't teach you something, some subject. And it doesn't make for a school. It's just a way of handling a question.

L.P. *We were talking about your fantasy of the Dallas school, which would be a depth psychology of the outer world, of the culture. Your colleagues there call it "cultural psychology."*

J.H. It begins in Freud. He saw the problem was in the civilization. Jung saw it too: the demonic, the psychotic is in collective consciousness. But they had no way of working on it, because they were still caught in the old idea of subjectivity and therapy of subjectivity. So they stopped short. I mean the basic analytical idea has always been you have to start with the individual to get to the civilization. Only by changing the consciousness of the individual can you affect the sickness of the civilization. If you want better medicine, put the doctors through an analysis, or better buildings, then get the architects into analysis. It's always starting with individuals: that's dogma, both Jungian and Freudian. Now I don't think it's at all enough to work on yourself, individually, or your relationships. What if the room you live in and work in is misshapen, made of bad materials, plastic clothes and poisoned air, with the ions flowing wrong, the sheets and pillows you sleep in made of petrochemicals in order to save ironing—not save sleeping—and the food is adulterated and the language you talk debased and the sounds mostly noise . . . the whole world is sick . . . and you can't put this right by having a good therapeutic dialogue or finding deeper meanings. It's not about meaning anymore; it's about survival.

L.P. *Do say more about this. It's terribly important.*

J.H. We have to realize where we are and where our consciousness is, which is: I am conscious and everything outside there is dead or at least doesn't have a soul, animals don't have souls, we know this from Descartes, from la Mettrie. It's also standard Christian stuff: only adult baptized humans have souls, have psyches, have subjectivity (that's standard Christian stuff until they get into the abortion question!), and we know it from Kant, too, that subjectivity is interior to us and the extended material world is "inorganic," dead, nothing blowing through it. We have even put ourselves as bodies "out there" into that dead inorganic world, even our own bodies! Ever since Vesalius's anatomy we have anatomized the body and studied it by means of a corpse: a structured machine of parts, so that medicine for the last four hundred years has made the body more and more dead. Of course we need machines for "understanding" our diseases, reading our bodies. Only machines can understand the body because it, too, has become a machine. Now, all this we know very well from Foucault, from van den Berg, from Merleau-Ponty. It means that the only one place where there is a subject, a consciousness, a reflective-ego-optical-observer is inside your head, your eyeballs. It's like God is outside creation in theology, altogether transcendent, so man, made in God's image, is outside, too, and everything out there in the street is a dead object. Something, a tree, may be lovely because it's made by God, but in itself it has no soul.

All this has created an incredible isolation of individuals, of consciousness, and a tremendous destruction of objects—plants, animals, lakes, rivers, soil, and also things; things are just dead so why not destroy them, they are dead anyway. (That many things live longer than we do, and we can't dispose of them so easily, that they are killing us, still hasn't created in us respect for them.

They still are dead according to our *Weltbild*. You see how powerful ideas are—they are not affected even by what we see every day, by the most overwhelming evidence.)

L.P. *Now where does soul come into this? So far you are complaining like the ecologists.*

J.H. Beyond the ecologists. Not just the "balance of nature," not just trees, that's the rhetoric of the Great Mother. I'm talking about things, *things*. Tables and cars and shoes and tin cans, plastic. We have to open our minds to the possibility of soul everywhere; we can't exclude things from it and love only nature. This means re-visioning the idea of soul before we can re-vision the idea of things. If we can get soul out of psychoanalysis, out of the Vatican, out of Kant and Descartes, and your own personal experience—all those places where it's been trapped or defined—and return it to the world, as the *anima mundi* of the Platonists then things, too, would be ensouled. When Plato used the word "psyche" it meant both at once: "my" soul in our sense and also soul as an objective world beyond "me" and in which I am. This is the world-soul, and I interpret it to mean the soul-in-the-world, and that everything has soul in some way or another. How would we perceive that? I look over there at that ashtray . . . what kind of soul has an ashtray or a stone or my shoelace? I think the only way we can get at the soul of the object is to think of it as a form or as a shape or a face, an image, and it displays its own image, its imagination. So it has a subjectivity. I don't mean that the shoelace experiences, remembers, feels, that it loves being tied into knots and hates hanging around loose—maybe it does. I don't mean that the ashtray waits for burning cigarette stubs with a masochistic pleasure—maybe it does. I don't know. But that isn't my point: I am not anthropomorphizing. It's more like a thing is a phenomenological presentation, with a depth, a complexity, a purpose, in a world of relations, with a memory, a history—so it is also a subjectivity. And if we look at it in this way we might begin to hear it. This isn't primitive animism either—that everything has a demon in it. It's an aesthetic appreciation of how things present themselves and that therefore they are in some way formed, ensouled, and are speaking to imagination.

This way of looking is a combination of the Neoplatonic *anima mundi* and pop art: that even a beer can or a freight car or a street sign has an image and speaks of itself beyond being a dead throwaway object.

L.P. *Pop-Neoplatonism! But another feature of pop and contemporary art is alienation in the world of objects, a world that is completely objectified, where imagination is confined to and limited by the objects. How can you make out of a world that is mostly objectified, a world that is ensouled again?*

J.H. You're saying objects are dominating individuals now. It's not that *objects* are dominating; it's a *view* of objects. It's the objective view that's dominating individuals. It's the view of my body as an object that I take to the doctor to have him tell me what's going on in it, so he puts my body into a machine, the machine tells the doctor something, the doctor translates that "objective" information to me; it's not that the object is dominating us. In fact, objects are completely disposable; we have no reverence for objects, we throw them away, we throw whole buildings away—disposable skyscrapers, good for twenty years and then you tear them down and throw them away, put up another one. It's the view that these are only objects that represses the soul of the object, and the return of the repressed comes back to make us feel overwhelmed by objects . . . as long as we think that only "we subjects" are in control and that that's what consciousness is, of course, then the objects become monstrous because we have created them as monsters; we have created them as golems or robots because we haven't considered the possibility that anything, any object (like for the old Egyptians, a thing is *"l'objet parlant"*) has its own echo beyond simply a material nature; the Egyptians, most cultures other than ours couldn't even separate a merely material nature. . . .

L.P. *This sounds like the surrealist or Dada view of objects, and it reverses completely the classical psychoanalytical conception of the subject-object relation.*

J.H. The psychoanalytical subject-object is just rehashed Western Cartesian stuff. Same old thing served up again. No; nothing to say about that because the moment you use those terms like "subject-object relation" they stick to you like tar—like blood—out, out, damned spot. I won't touch that model of thought.

L.P. *Then just go on talking about objects.*

J.H. I don't even like that word. I object to it. Hah! It's a general term that robs a thing of its specific name and face. Like calling people, you, me, subjects. See how we have to examine our language all the time to keep from being trapped. We have to shift the whole paradigm of subject and object around, to think for example that they are looking at us, not only that we are looking at them. That moves the entire question of who's the object of what.... Of course, I'm thinking again of modern art, when they try to "let the material speak," just a big piece of plastic or rusty iron or whatever it is, it is to let the thing show itself phenomenally, to show us its face. Now, that physiognomy of the thing puts one into a relationship with the thing.

L.P. *We usually use objects we ourselves have not made, and we are technologically dependent on objects. This gives a feeling that objects are totally foreign to us. Only children try to use objects the way you have described.*

J.H. We eat apples we didn't make ourselves and talk to children we didn't make ourselves. It has nothing to do with creating the thing yourself as an extension of yourself. In fact, this very idea that objects are extensions of ourselves, expressions of ourselves, tools, the whole Darwinian anthropological view of objects as tools starts with the Western ego, the will. So, let's turn it around: start with the object. Doesn't the tool in your hand teach you how to use it? Take a needle: my eyes, my fingers have to adjust to that needle's eye and pass the thread through it. The needle teaches me a strict discipline, a refinement of eye-hand coordination. If I do it wrong, the needle pricks me or gets out of my grip. Things are our "masters" in that sense. And when you kick the TV set or curse the car because it doesn't work, it's because we are being bad students. We don't want to learn—and we learn only when things break down, I mean not just things, I mean our bodies, our psyches. We learn when there is an interruption. The problem of these things, objects, technology, is a psychological problem, first of all. It is the idea of these objects as merely objective dead matter, that's the cause of the problem, not the tool.

Let me tell you a story: a friend of mine years ago was in Egypt, in a village, in the Nile delta. A peasant wanted his wristwatch. This friend knew Egypt somewhat, and he was able to find out just how this man saw, understood, the wristwatch. It was a power; it had mana—not because you could tell time by it, but because Western people, Europeans, would be casually walking along or just doing something or other, and they'd raise their arms and glance at their watches, and then suddenly change their expression, suddenly look upset, start walking much faster, or even change direction one hundred eighty degrees. Now any amulet that could do *that* to you, must have a God in it. Now, my friend believed the watch was dead, it was only his tool; but the Egyptian saw the watch as a subject, an even more important subject in some remarkable way than its "owner." But we don't need these anthropological anecdotes. Take your own typewriter; as you work with your typewriter, it becomes yours and you "love it," won't have any other. When you're using a complicated automobile, it becomes *your* automobile; you recognize its subjectivity. So don't believe we can get around this question of objective consciousness that creates objects as objects. We don't start with an object. We start with *objective consciousness* that considers these things out there as objects. Our objectifying consciousness makes them objects. But as soon as we enter into conversation with them, live with them imaginatively, our objectifying consciousness changes and they no longer are dead objects.

L.P.   *How could this return of the soul to the things of the street affect psychotherapy?*

J.H.   Let's take a husband and wife in a modern suburb, and they fight about drink and money and in-laws and love and little habits. Then he goes to analysis and she goes to analysis and they work on the relationship, and they are good sincere patients who try—group therapy, team or office therapy, family therapy, sex therapy—they get it all together as human decent people. They may even go to Church. And still there is a terrible misery going on, because the room in which they're set, its low ceiling, thin

hollow doors, the bed, the dishes, the TV programs, the maga-
zines, the light tubes, the furniture they have around them, and
so on and so on, the whole world of material things, verbal
things, institutional things in which their marriage is set is nasty,
brutish, ugly, cheap, shoddy, vicious—without soul at all. Fake.
How can they possibly straighten out their situation if the whole
stage set including the lines in the script are fake?

Wait—let me go on: Psychotherapy is something very strange
in a world like this. It used to rely on a bourgeois world that had
certain values and kinds of things, qualities, that had to be seen
through, with irony, with skepsis. See the repressed. But that
world has disappeared. The politics, language, education, institutions that upheld the marriage disappeared, the buildings, streets,
lights, food, words, tables and chairs are gone: but psychotherapy
still works as if all that scenery is still around, analyzing the marriage with theories of 1920 in a 1980 set. Unless psychotherapy
takes into account the sickness of the world, it can never really
work, because the *anima mundi* is sick now. Pathology is "out
there." You feel it on the highway, you feel it in the car, you feel
it in your sense that something is out of tune, false or ugly or
unemotional or without soul or vapid or sexless, tasteless. How
can psychoanalysis justify itself, two people in a room talking?

Jungians say the justification is in the work of analysis with an
individual soul: transformation of the individual, and as that individual transforms, it affects the whole world. The Marxist
would say, There's no justification; you have to correct the whole
world; it has to be set up again on a correct basis. But their "correct" basis is utterly mechanical, narrow—and fake, too. I think
that psychoanalysis hasn't taken the world into account. Psychoanalysis has to get out of the consulting room and analyze all
kinds of things. You have to see that the buildings are anorexic,
you have to see that the language is schizogenic, that "normalcy"
is manic, and medicine and business is paranoid. You have to see
what's actually happening, the distortions. The whole world has
to become a patient so to speak. . . .

L.P. *But what can be done?*

J.H. Well, to start simply with the couple who were just fighting
in that imagined modern suburb in their little "development" box,

the moment they realize that it's not only them—"You said...."
"It's your fault...." "And my mother...." "And your father...."
"And our sex-life...." "And you spend too much"—that it is
more than their personal troubles, more even than their dreams
and their histories as people; what is wrong with their marriage,
with them, and their lives has to do with their TV, with the
words they use for fighting, the chairs they sit in when they are
arguing, the room itself. Then they can wake up. They see the
cave. Then their relationship is suddenly placed in a context
where they are not enemies against each other but can become
collaborators in waking up to the world that is driving them crazy, projecting on to them its own suffering and making them
suffer, so that the only way they have been able to find to live in
this soulless world is to become soulless too by drinking or by
numbing yourself to a piece of plastic with pills or stuffing yourself silly on food.

If we can see we are in that film *Fahrenheit 451,* or that film of
Bergman's about Berlin, *The Serpent's Egg* . . . It's already here.
. . . *1984* happened ten years ago, fifteen years ago. People say,
"Oh, Orwell was off. Here it is, the 1980s and it's not like he
said." But we are already in that consciousness without knowing
it, which is just what *1984* is about: being unconscious of what is
happening to you from the world. The destruction of language,
the paranoid perversion of value, the impersonality of relationships and the romanticism that we can be saved by personal love,
the feeling that the system is bigger than any of us and we can't
do anything about it, the television is watching us, the things
around are "bugged," we become the objects and they the subjects—but in a dead way, a wrong way—that's all *1984,* and it is
here.

L.P.   *It sounds like the past, too, not just* 1984. *It sounds like the
concentration camp.*

J.H.   Oh, yes; that's right. The fascination with the Holocaust as
they call it, as if it were a new product or something, is a displacement. The Holocaust wasn't in the 1940s only. It's going on
now. Not just that the world will go up in fire, but that we are
living in a psychic concentration camp, in the sense that we are
passively accepting the soulless world. So when they debate

about the Jews—"How could they let themselves just be gassed like that. Why did no one, or so few do anything?" Well, that's a displacement. We have to ask ourselves, Why don't we now, *today, do something* about the soullessness we live among? And that's what I mean by seeing the psychopathology in the world and finding a way of working with that *as a psychologist.*

L.P. *There's an answer which is the terrorist's answer: who cares if I'm going to kill a human life? It may not be the ideal, the answer; but that human life is already rotten or dead and the whole system, everything, has to go into complete and total change. Only terrorism can make us feel the terror of this concentration camp, this holocaust, this 1984, that you describe. That would be one kind of terrorist's answer.*

J.H. I don't know the terrorists. I don't know how they feel or see the world. But this imaginary terrorist you just acted, yes, is close to what I am saying. Only I want to deal with it *psychologically*—and that is a huge difference!

L.P. *How do you and the terrorist—imaginary terrorist—agree?*

J.H. First of all, let's take that word "terror" as a reaction to the terror already in the world, the terrible, terrifying condition of its soul. The terror was there before the terrorists. They made it conscious—I don't mean that *they* are conscious, but that they made terror conscious, and so, for all their awfulness, they are part of the consciousness-raising, the therapy that is going on outside of the consulting room. We have to face things we never would have faced. They are awful, but still they have forced us to lift a repression.

L.P. *How do you mean the terror is already there in the world unconsciously?*

J.H. If you had been in a concentration camp in the forties and the doctors took out your womb, that would be a war crime, wouldn't it? All right, and now more than half of the women over forty in the United States have their wombs removed. Imagine that! Every other woman over forty you pass in the street in the United States has no uterus. Hysterectomies are performed more than appendectomies and tonsillectomies. It's America's favorite operation. This is terrifying, terrible—it's not forced on the women as in a concentration camp. They come willingly: it's "good for you." Or take Germany today: one out of seven people—that means millions—take sleeping pills of some kind *every* night. This is *Fahrenheit 451; 1984,* . . . don't you see?

Of course, today we don't live in concentration camps, literally, with barbed wire and SS guards. But if we go on imagining those camps of the forties as the *only kind* of terror, then we miss the actual horrors that are perpetrated every day—whether with toxic dumps and industrial pollutants or with drug prescriptions or with those hysterectomies. Even if the women collude with their surgeons and want the operation, it is still a horror. The clitoridectomies in some African societies or the binding of Chinese feet in the Mandarin culture were horrors, terrors in fact, even if the women "wanted" these operations. Terror doesn't depend only on whether what's done to you is "voluntary" or not—that's a big part of it, of course, and I'm not denying that in the 1940s in Germany cruelty and force were used. Cruelty and force can happen in ways that are not felt as cruelty and force—but still they are cruelty and force. For instance, we know from studying what goes on in schizogenic families that the terror is there even if it's not perceived. At least then, in the 1940s, we weren't already so anesthetized, already so unconscious that the victims didn't sense what was happening. Maybe it's worse today since we don't even sense it. Instead we have this huge displacement on abortion, the right to life. Never mind the fetus; what about the women over forty? What about what's happening—the terror of which we are unconscious—in our everyday anesthetized lives! And this is only the medical aspect, and a tiny bit of it.

Look at the world of buildings: look at all that has been blown up and torn down, everything solid and well made and with memory—now if that happened in the forties, and it did happen—Dresden, Coventry, Rotterdam, Warsaw, all over—it was called bombing and destruction, and we mourned the loss of our cities. Now we call it development, and the people who do it are called "developers" and "planners." This is Orwell: *1984.* Then it was terror: now, of course, people aren't firebombed and killed, but the civilization—the world of things that are their repositories of memory and beauty and love—these are gone, and I think this is a terror, an unconscious terror, an even worse terror to live in a city that has been destroyed and yet looks marvelous and new. The soul feels its loss but it can't tell what's wrong. It's schizogenic. We are getting two signals at once, because the actual destruction that is terrible is given wonderful names like "development" "urban renewal"—and then we wonder why the cities with their marvelous buildings and developments are full of crime, as if it were the fault of social factors or unemployment or fatherless families. Well, the crime begins in those buildings, on the drawing boards and planning commissions. One crime begets another.

L.P. *Aren't you exaggerating? Aren't you neglecting population growth that needs new buildings and the social improvements that come with tearing down the slums? And aren't you grossly generalizing about old buildings being all good and new buildings being all bad?*

J.H. Of course I'm exaggerating. That's the best way to enter into the extremist mentality: not by taking the opposite stance of reasonable good sense. If you become classic with me, sure enough I'll become romantic. Right now we are attempting to enter the anarchist fantasy, the nihilist fantasy of terrorism. And I'm trying to place it as a reaction to a world-soul that is in terror, from all that has been done to its materialization in things. Not just by developers and planners, but by Christianity and Descartes and Newton and by science and the universities . . . our whole tradition has declared matter and material things to be evil and dead to begin with. You've studied philosophy; you know how much serious time is spent proving the reality of the external world. Imagine having to prove what every animal knows! You know that our main tradition says the world has no qualities whatsoever—no color, no taste, no texture, no temperature—and some of that tradition even denies its existence if we aren't there to perceive it. Ascetic world-denial, world destruction going on every day in our philosophy classes. Terrorism and nihilism are already in our Western world view, so the terrorists are the incarnation of the nihilism that is inherent to our system of thinking. Its roots lie in the Christian *Weltbild,* so, of course, a symbolic act of nihilism is to kill the Pope, whose shadow is this nihilism in Christianity. Psychic syndromes of this vast proportion present themselves with that sort of massive demonstration. But symptoms—remember what we learned from Freud and from Jung—are always purposeful. They are compromises with the problem, even attempts to solve it.

L.P.   *You are placing terrorism right within Christianity, then?*

J.H.   Yes, I am. We have to stop being so pious! Just historically, don't you think the Christian Church knows a thing or two about terror: the fourth century, the persecution of heretics. Goodness! If only the Christians could see terrorism as *theirs,* at least partly, if they could begin to own it, then some changes could come about. If you sit outside the Christian world, as an American Indian, as an Egyptian in the fourth century, as a Jew most anytime—Christianism looks pretty terrifying. Or just take the Japanese at Nagasaki; who brought them that bomb? Christianity has a terrible shadow, and we have to begin somehow to take it into ourselves.

L.P.   *Let's say these terrorists whom we are imagining—and there must be many kinds of them in fact—are idealists, and because they enact an apocalyptic resolution to materialism, they remain au fond Christians.*

J.H.   This is not only Italian, not only Christian. I remember a student of religion telling me about his T.M., his meditation. Somebody in the seminar said, "What about the political world?" He said, "That doesn't matter. Computers can run the political world, the whole country, much more efficiently, and that frees us to pursue enlightenment with meditation." Do you see the complete harmony between central dictatorship, fascism, political callousness, and the self-centeredness of the spiritual point of view? It opened my eyes: I saw the present cults of meditation not so gentle, not so harmless as they like to be, but a vicious bunch of totalitarians. They can't see the individual—which you see only if you look for soul, look with soul. They can't see an individual person, let alone an individual thing. And the terrorist shooting a man coming out his front door, shooting him in the knees, is not seeing that man at all. He is in his spiritual meditation, he is actually a religious fanatic.

L.P. *Sometimes they act their mission as if it were a sacred martyrdom, as if they were saints of the Antichrist. However, as you say, they have brought our whole society to recognize something: its invisible, inherent terror, and its soullessness. I saw in Germany on a wall: "Wo ist meine Seele, die Bundesrepublik hat Sie getötet." [Where is my soul, the Federal Republic has killed her.]*

J.H. Before the terrorism, in the revolution of '68, the students put on the wall at the Sorbonne: *Imagination au pouvoir*. But imagination hasn't got power—it can't rule in that sense. It has to rule within our acts, each act, as the image in the act. I think they have actually lost their imagination and so they think in big words like "Power" and "*Bundesrepublik*." This is totalitarian thinking, monotheistic thinking. An All-doer, a Supreme One that is at fault and who can set it straight like a guru. The reverse of this One is Nothing. Nihilism. They don't even have images of how the world should be, images of Utopia. It would be terribly sad if it weren't so dreadful. They are like those mystics who have wiped out imagination to live in the dark night of the spirit, and their *via negativa* shoots you in the knees—the knees, the very place of kneeling, of genuflection, bending before images. We have to tie terrorism to its roots in our religious consciousness. A terrorist is the product of our education that says that fantasy is not real, that says aesthetics is just for artists, that says soul is only for priests, imagination is trivial or dangerous and for crazies, and that reality, what we must adapt to, is the external world, and that world is dead. A terrorist is a result of this whole long process of wiping out the psyche. Corbin said to me one time, "What is wrong with the Islamic world is that it has destroyed its images, and without these images that are so rich and so full in its tradition, they are going crazy because they have no containers for their extraordinary imaginative power." His work with mystic philosophical texts, the texts that reestablish the imaginal world, can be seen as political action of the first order: it was meeting terrorism, fanaticism, nihilism right at its roots in the psyche. But Khomeini won: Corbin died in October and Khomeini started back in December.

L.P. *Then your work, too, with active imagination, activating the images, could also be seen as counterterrorism, and although your work seems only introverted, only to ignore the world, it is really deeply political.*

J.H. Political consciousness isn't only in the political world. Doesn't it have to begin in the soul? Don't we have to move things *there,* fundamentally, but not in regard to the "self" only, in regard to the world? This terrorist, this imaginary figure who is blowing things up because his apocalyptic vision tells him the world needs to be blown up for its true redemption—he is still with Nietzsche, not really pagan, not really polytheistic, because he—or she, oh, yes, *she* too—does not recognize the world as alive with soul, that things are faces, voices, persons, and that the world soul is suffering and you have to find a way to this patient, not just execute it with a bomb. The terrorist, too, takes the world out there as a dead object: so blow up the Bologna railroad stations.

L.P. *That was a purely politically motivated act.*

J.H. Whatever the conscious motivations, the result is the destruction of the city.

L.P. *And the people . . .*

J.H. Of course, life. But human life isn't the only place of soul. It's just that failure, that neglect to see the sacredness of the constructed world, too, made with human hands and human imagination and love—what we have been doing on this earth for thousands of years—that makes the world out there disposable, obsolescent, trash. We need to save that trash through a revolution in our perception of it. A revolution in sensitivity, an aesthetic revolution . . . becoming more and more sensitive, rather than more and more violent. Of course, violence can be a sensitive reaction, like striking out when somebody touches your raw skin, but I think the violence now is not that. It seems more programmatic, a reaction out of deadness.

L.P. *You don't want to recycle the trash like an ecologist or bury the trash and build on top of it like big business. You want to save the trash . . .*

J.H. . . . like a therapist. Therapy has been working with the trash for years.

L.P. *Your aesthetic revolution still sounds like Dada.*

J.H. Like Dada, yes, but far more urgent than in 1920. Dada is a good model because it's not tragic, it's not Christian—it's too funny. And it's not programmatic and self-important. No idealism, no Transcendental Meditation, no crossing over Jordan into the promised land—no promises and no land. Land fantasies just release a swarm of bulldozers, those utopian development fantasies: let's build it all new. No. Dada stays with what is and turns it upside down, inside out. We have to watch out for Jerusalems and just more fanaticism. And we can't just cross the river into the trees, return to nature, the greening of America. We have to cross the river into the street, like Dada.

L.P. *How? How does your aesthetic revolution proceed?*

J.H. We are getting inflated now. Once it's called "your revolution" . . . no, no . . . besides, even speaking like this about Dada begins to make a program of something that is essentially unprogrammatic.

L.P. *Seriously; how do we enact this vision of returning soul to the world?*

J.H. That question is too much to handle. It's what I am working on now, and for at least two years. I can't summarize it. I can't even begin.

L.P. *Don't try to explain it. Just tell me what you are imagining.*

J.H. Depth psychology . . . well, all psychology, clinical, experimental, even social, isn't concerned with the sensuous relation with the world. It's left out the aesthetic. Yet that's what we are: we are sensuously imagining animals. The first thing the psyche does is make sensuous images. So why not imagine a psychology that starts there, in the aesthetic nature of human being and the aesthetic nature of the world which displays itself in sense events, to the senses, and the first reaction is to live a thing as a sense image. Things have skins and faces and smells. Things speak to us and that's what I mean, first of all, by aesthetics, speaking to the senses, and having a sensitivity to that skin or sheen of things. Now that would be a revolution. It would give the world back to its soul, and let the soul out of our private personal subjective idea of it. We might then love the world and not be in terror of it. Or want to kill it, blow it up. Psychoanalysis has kept us in a personal subjectivism and ignored the five senses which connect us to things, to everything that's not "me."

Most Western psychology has been abstract psychology, a second-level psychology, conceptual and explanatory. But we could turn to the world of smell and language and color and crafts and songs and nature and food—the world that the Italian Renaissance was concerned with, and we could rebuild psychology on an aesthetic basis. And in the Renaissance this sensuous world was immediately connected with the mythical world of Gods and Planets. In other words, I am imagining an archetypal psychology that is both mythical *and* sensuously refined *and* imagistic *and* animal—immediate—all at once. I warned you this was hard to talk about. But psychoanalysis has got to take the world back into its view . . . the everyday concrete world of the senses. I want a base for psychology in what I called some years ago "the poetic basis of mind," in the sensuous imagination that is also in actual things, in the street—not in the abstractions of psychoanalysis and certainly not in pseudoscience, those abstract literalisms called "body" experience or physiological mechanisms about brains. This move from science and literalism to aesthetics is really far away from Jung and Freud and their nineteenth-century concern with science, and their consequent romantic concern with the subjective soul which for them was localized in individual persons—the same old view of the Western Christian tradition. That's why recently I've been more interested in, and wrote a long essay on, Alfred Adler—his *Gemeinschaftsgefühl,* or social interest or community feeling, moves psychology into a worldly concern, out of the private consulting room. Adler died right out in the street. What a powerful blessing.

9 WRITING

J.H. You asked me about my "intellectual development," and I dodged away because it shows in what one has written; there it is, right there, printed. All that one writes is autobiography and particularly in psychology. Psychology is a presentation of one's psychic concerns, concerns in the sense of "what have you caught," complexes, traps.

L.P. *You have written eight papers on the puer theme. The large book,* Puer Papers, *collects four of them and seems to have induced others to write on the same theme with you. Is the complex of eternal youth, the young God, of being a boy of the spirit, therefore one of your own "traps"?*

J.H. The puer work began in 1967. I was forty-one—hardly a boy in years, but an American after all, and it takes us longer than most! Anyway, my passion was to write a defense of the puer because I felt insulted by what Jungians were saying about this archetype. I had swallowed the Jungian view that puer meant mother complex, weakness, fancy, aestheticism, not in touch with reality, up-in-the-air, donjuanism . . . about fifteen negative words used about *puer aeternus.* Having lived my life, or part of my life, within that mythical structure, it seemed to me that it was being abused. It really hit me, angered me, and I began then my own enormous piece of work on the puer archetype, a phenomenology. Some pieces of it have been published in the last ten years. Now, that was partly a biographical vindication of my own mythical structure.

L.P. *Or was it a mythical vindication of your biographical structure?*

J.H. You're putting it reductively. I'm putting it from the viewpoint of the puer itself: we start in myth and live myth in biography. And that's why you have to read my myths—my books—to get my biography. The puer writings are far beyond my own mother complex and father complex, my own puer structure. That structure is a gift, too, for it gave me the chance to have insight into the problem beyond me, the big problem that angered me so. There was this sense that something dreadful was happening in the midst of this Jungian psychology that meant so much to me. A new repression was happening and no one saw it. A whole spiritual possibility in young men and in the spirit of the culture was being destroyed by the condemnation of the puer. It meant that we were attacking our own creative possibility. Later I felt the same way about hysteria: something was happening to women and to Dionysus in this term "hysteria."

L.P. *You published on women and hysteria in 1969 in your* Eranos *lecture and then later it formed a major section of* The Myth of Analysis. *In 1969 the feminist revolution was entering consciousness. Your work was important for that because you showed the misjudgments of psychiatry against women (hysteria) and the misjudgments of classical studies against Dionysus.*

J.H. These angers were something very deep. There was an outrage and, looking back, I think my own spirit, my ram-headed Mars, was finally coming up and out of a long sleep, a kind of long anima-sleep, you know, autoerotic self-concern, symptoms, wanting to be loved, wanting success.

L.P. *But you seem always to have been angry or to work out of outrage, at least in your writings:* Suicide and the Soul *(1964) is an attack on medicine and "Betrayal."* . . .

J.H. I trust my anger. It's my favorite demon. Writing and anger go together.

L.P. *How did* Re-Visioning Psychology *begin? Those were the famous Terry Lectures at Yale. Jung gave them in 1937, and Rebecca West, Paul Tillich, Paul Ricoeur. . . .*

J.H. Oh, yes, and many others like Dewey. But that's the inflating part. I used to go to the Ticino for five-day stretches to write. I began to just write things, I didn't have a purpose in mind: but I began to see the importance of psychopathology in the whole psychoanalytical business, for all of the work begins in pathology. And slowly I began to write about what we really are doing in this work, why pathology is so important, and the idea of seeing into and seeing through. So I had these thoughts in my head and some on paper already in 1970. That was the period when I had stopped practicing. Stopped for two years. Maybe I had written my way out of being a disciple who had been "trained."

I wasn't burned out as they say now. I was embarrassed, ashamed. I just hated the psychoanalytical business too much and myself in it—like a scalding or an acid or something that made it impossible. I had also been in a scandal and that broke many of my relationships. I saw they were frauds, I was a fraud. Breakdown. A whole world collapsed. There's some biography for you. . . . All of these things went into *Re-Visioning Psychology*, I guess, looking back. Oh, yes, in March 1969 I went to London with Lopez and Valerie, who became his wife, and Pat, who became my wife, and I was working on the Dionysus theme, and we went to the Warburg Institute and the British Museum—and all these new thoughts about Western psychology came pouring into my head, and I was writing little notes to myself on everything I could find, thoughts about the Gods, about polytheism, about images, the Renaissance, I wanted to find out who were Ficino, and Gemisto Pletho, really. I suddenly saw a foundation. Other things were no longer interesting—I remember walking into the Asian section of the Warburg Library and walking out of it saying, that's finished. I can close that off. What a relief. Now you see all this together became the Terry Lectures, *Re-Visioning Psychology*.

L.P. *We could date the beginning of archetypal psychology, perhaps, to that visit to London in 1969. If that is so, it brings out several characteristics of archetypal psychology itself. The turn away from the East and toward the South: Renaissance Italy. Then, it was a cultural move, in the Warburg Institute, rather than a clinical one—your earlier writings were on emotion and suicide. Then, too, you made this trip with friends. It was already at the beginning a group participation, moved by anima or by eros.*

J.H. This sounds all true, but it sounds too historical. If we start dating the moment when books form, then they become like the

Battle of Hastings or something. Besides, it's too neat, and you can't separate culture and clinic. But as far as friends go, and not being alone, yes, that is true. Still, you could also say archetypal psychology began in 1966—nine hundred years after the Battle of Hastings!—while I was working on my first Eranos lecture, and I was very much alone with it. The problem I was tackling was creativity: what is psychological creativity, what makes for a *psychologically* creative person. When you go into that notion, creativity, you find six or seven basic views of it. As I began organizing these views I found they fell into archetypal baskets. There was a puer notion—free and new and original: a Great Mother basket—growth and fertility; a senex basket . . .

L.P. *It's all in* The Myth of Analysis *now . . .*

J.H. . . . and so on, and these were archetypal perspectives, and none of them was wrong and none of them better than any other. They were archetypal backgrounds to how we know something. That made me see that the problem of knowledge, of epistemology, has archetypal fantasies as its base. These archetypal fantasies are working all the time, not just in therapy, not just in relationships, but in the way we think about and know things. The polytheistic psychology of *Re-Visioning Psychology* had already begun in 1966.

L.P. *A very strange book.*

J.H. A strange book. Well, there were all sorts of attempts to break the mold of a psychology book. There's the self-reflectiveness and the attempts to keep the same thematics and the same images going, and also the attempt to disassociate the author from the book. The author is a "persona" in the novelistic sense within the book.

L.P. *He disappears in it and from it.*

J.H. How do you mean that?

L.P. *Well, I remember the ending of the book where you practically have a sort of pageant with all the contents . . .*

J.H. Walking away . . .

L.P.   ...*Walking away and disappearing in nothingness; and all that survives is anima. Well, anima is also just nothing, in a way. And there is a conscious effort—a rhetorical effort never to let the contents be literal. They can be taken literally for the sake of the argument up to a certain point, but then you drop them, you unmask them. And you say, "I've been meaning this until now, but now just jump into a . . .void."*

J.H.   How do you write a book which is to present a mass of ideas seriously and yet not be caught by the old mode of presentation of serious ideas?

L.P.   *Don't use literal arguments.*

J.H.   Well, it's polemical.

L.P.   *It's full of polemics. But the weight lifting is fully rhetorical. Your style requires that you put a set of ideas against another set of ideas.*

J.H.   Yes, it's full of polemical argument, but argument, as you say, is used within a rhetorical mode rather than within the old style of opposition or contradictory thinking, proof and disproof.

L.P.   *To read your work for proof would be to read you quite wrongly.*

J.H.   That's right. One of the remarks about the book, on the back cover, is "Here is a whole book about the soul without ever mentioning a single human person—except historical persons, authors." There's not a single case, a literal case, in the book. Which was again an attempt to free the soul from its identification with personality. The Greeks hadn't the idea "person." They didn't have the word "person." That book is written in the style that you would have to get into if you were in the Renaissance or Greece—in my mind. It doesn't use the fundamental categories that are used by twentieth-century psychology, which says, if you are going to talk about the psyche, you have to talk about people, cases, sociology. That's not so. The Greek Plato talked about psyche, without locating it in a case or person.

The word "person" is something that Augustine gave us, really. It comes with Christianity. It isn't that person isn't an important idea, it's just that if you're trying to get out of a certain mode of thought, you have to get out of all those ways that we get trapped in that thought. So, there are, on purpose, no cases, no examples. There is, on purpose, no evidence to prove a point. There is, on purpose, no ontological basis. That is: this book is the soul, the soul is the substance. And everything's built out of this soul substance. There's no attempt to build a structure for it to rest on or make a system apart from it. The friend who wrote the index for *Re-Visioning Psychology* said, "How do you do an index for a novel?" Because there aren't those concrete noun-subjects that make for an index. There are, as you say, rhetorical ways of expressing things that don't become topics in the usual sense. And the same with *The Dream and the Underworld* (1979). That book tries to explain how myth is a basis—but it's a basis that disappears the moment you try to base something on it.

L.P.   *I find that index in* Re-Visioning *very useful, and the footnotes very useful. If the footnotes were not there, if the index was not there, I think your book could be a piece of pagan apologetics. It could have been written—well, in the fourth century.*

J.H.   Marvelous! The book has its own little biography. The first model of the book that I sent the editor were the lectures at Yale, which could be read through in an evening. They were four one-hour lectures and could be read just as spoken. Then there were the notes, which would be very rich, full of commentary, on the lectures—the second level of the text. Then the third level was a collection of appendices. I had written about seventeen appendices on basic ideas all through the book, expanding them. The editor said it was far too complicated. Already then there was this idea of commentaries on commentaries. I thought the book could be read on different levels. People could use it for what they wanted. Eventually those appendices went into the body of the book in smaller print as "excursions." You could skip the excursions or you could read them, and they stood out by themselves. All the way along, there was this "how-to-do" the forming of the book, both by the editor and by myself. The problem of form was there all along.

L.P.   *The form is very firm though. That is not where the strangeness lies.*

J.H. Well, it took a long time to get that firmness. I ought to say the book was turned down by Yale University Press and by another publisher, too. And some of that firmness came from the editors who helped my sentence formations which, of course, means my thought. Editors, you know, are therapists of the sentence. Nothing is more intimate than the way your thought comes into words. That's your very soul, and editors, if they are good, know how to do precise work with your written soul.

L.P. *It's still a difficult book to translate just because it depends so on the style.*

J.H. I am so grateful to translators. It's such incredibly undervalued work. The translator has to enter into the same kind of mind, worship somehow at the same altar. I once knew the American translator of Mallarmé and Corbière. He used to sit on the graves to get into their souls. If you don't phrase it right, get the right rhythms, my book won't make sense, or worse, it will get turned into conceptual arguments, the old mode again.

L.P. *Yet, it isn't presented fuzzily. It's quite clear, you know.*

J.H. Thanks to the process of rewriting, of editing. It's an alchemical clarifying, a "whitening." *Re-Visioning Psychology* has been used in America in many kinds of classes: abnormal psychology, philosophy, religion, it's been used in art classes and film classes, in post modern consciousness courses. . . .The students who have to use the book often feel bitter or complain because they want to know what he's trying to say, they want it *explained.* It's hard for them because they are being asked to read differently. Writing it, I was only trying to be clear. My struggle is to hold the horse, not to make it fly. It's very hard to be clear, for me; maybe that's why often I go to extremes. I keep feeling each thing has to be turned on its head so that it can't fall back to where it was before. And each idea has to be moved as far as it can go so that the others can move, too. If you let one clichéd thought get in, it affects all the others. At the same time I wanted to be as free, to let it rip. It isn't just to be free, but to be free *and to work it out.* So I didn't censor very much.

I remember a certain passage that I cut out because it seemed too far-fetched: about the Gods being in things, in the streets, and in buildings, and so on and so forth. I cut that out. And of course, that's exactly the thought—the reanimation of the world—that I am now working in 1980. And it's extraordinary how one's thought is legitimate. You censor your own thought because you think, This is too crazy. Where'd this come from: this idea, that the shapes of things are the faces of the Gods? And I remember cutting it out because I couldn't establish it, connect it, in any way. It was connected, but my conscious critical mind couldn't see it. And I wasn't able to elaborate it properly. Imagine that! The idea of the reanimation of the world was already happening in my hands when I was writing six years ago. I think that desire to go as far as you possibly can go is what writing is for. I tried to do that also in *The Dream and the Underworld*. It's absolutely crazy—parts of that book. When I say crazy, I mean there's an aspect beyond your ability to rationally justify what you've said. Letting it go doesn't mean you don't try to hold it back. Both together. Crazy and clear both. That's the Apollonic necessity: to keep it clear. Concise and well-formed. It's crucial.

L.P.   *Your way of writing seems deliberately irregular and thera-peutic. You are so often going off sideways. Like therapy, you don't ban anything from your writing. You let so much, maybe too much, come in. Very often it is difficult to get a real hold of one idea. One thing can be said: one cannot learn a thing from your writings, like one cannot learn a thing from a sermon, or an "orazione," but just "save one's soul," agree or disagree, and ad-mire. So one goes through your writings with their slack pas-sages, their peaks, the masses of erudition, the literary aperçus and flourishes, the historical knowledge . . . Do you deliberately write in this style?*

J.H.   It's not a plan, it's *me*; for example, gathering a lot of mate-rial, spending a lot of time on what you might call the standard conscious tradition, . . . and then comes that leap out of it, or movement through it, turning it around on its head. Now that move is psychologically deliberate. See, I don't believe you can move—and we've said this all through this interview—unless you take all the baggage with you. So—if you are going to write about Pan. . . .

L.P.   *Pan; that's a good example. Your* Essay on Pan *that had such popularity in Italy—you know it was a best seller—is written*

*first as an accompaniment of a traditional piece of German schol-
arship. That's why it opens so slowly—and then you leap out.*

J.H.   The whole leap depends on the slow pace at the beginning,
like a long flat run before a broad jump. First, you've got to enter
into everybody's Pan. *Then,* you can move that standard conscious tradition. Anything that you want to move has to start
where it is, in its stuckness. That involves erudition—probably
too much erudition. One wants to get stuck in the history, the
material, the knowledge, even relish it: a library is a restaurant. I
gobble everything up, and it gives me appetite to go on. I
wouldn't really know what I want to say about Pan until I've
eaten a lot so that my writing is part of a digesting and spitting
out what other people say and getting caught by the whole complex of it. It's like therapy: you need to get caught in the other
person's complex in order to move that complex. If a woman says
to me "You're doing just what my husband does. You're cutting
me off when I talk, you're turning away, you react to me as if I'm
the greatest bore in the world the moment I try to tell you an
idea I have." I'll say, "Thank God!, now we are where it really is."
Meaning that I'm caught in the psychic material—"I'm enacting
the very complex that you've been living at home." That's the
complex. If I become your father or your brother or your husband or whatever, we're now in that situation where we may be
able to move it. Now that's the same thing I do when I write:
deliberately spending time in the old place. Then suddenly seeing through the old place.

L.P.   *Why is your style so uneven?*

J.H.   Let's say the unevenness is because of two things. One is
that's the way I am, mixed. Mixed, *meshugge.* Second, it's a Her-
metic mode. In alchemy, mercury is the color of green *and* yellow, all things that are mixed, all things that are double, or not
the same from moment to moment, and so on. I would rather
write a beautiful essay. You know—just fluent. I can't write simple fluent prose. To justify my mess, let's say it belongs to a polytheistic mode, a psychological mode, because all the complexes
are talking and have their say. The old professor has his footnotes, and the puer has his flights: there are all sorts of purple

little flights going on, wings and flowers, and those things. And there is an attempt to relate what is happening in the book to the reader's own misery. You see, I don't think this essay should be written by this complex or that essay written by that complex necessarily. Why not let various voices speak in the same piece of work?

L.P. *So, it is not so much unevenness, but letting go of the monotheistic style in psychological writing.*

J.H. That's right—the writing in the journals and textbooks is very puritan: all abstractions and nothing baroque allowed. It's utterly up-front, nothing is ever insinuated. You don't evoke the reader's fantasy, you don't even allow your own fantasy. Single-minded and everything coming to a neat linear "conclusion." Psychology has tried all century long to be scientific and now it speaks like science and is trapped in that boring language. No adjectives. No adverbs. They are too "subjective" because science says they are personal opinions and don't belong to the objective world. So, psychology cuts out the adjectives—and the subjunctive, and the metaphor. . . .

You write, "She's a thirty-four-year-old woman, a hundred and forty-two pounds, five feet six, paranoid schizophrenia." But you'd never say something as Dickens would, "her eyes, flecked with silver, slyly averting her glance, falling into silence as if to attend assiduously to her own thoughts." We need to look at our patients as Visconti, as Fellini would. You rarely read now in America a careful description of the patient as you read in older psychiatry books of Bleuler and Kraepelin. Now our language is statistical prediction—a hundred people classified so-and-so, so many will get better within this period with this drug, and so on. You don't get the individual descriptive eye any longer, the clinician's eye, the bedside eye, Flaubert's eye. We don't trust our own eyes and haven't any language for what we see anyhow, so we give a Rorschach test, a Minnesota inventory test. That language is clean, objective. Result: we've lost our language for describing the very material we work with—people. This suppression of language makes most psychology books deadly. They don't speak about the psyche and they don't speak to the psyche. No complexity. Which means that the great psychological books are either novels or plays or biographies, even philosophy; or they're Freud's mode of writing. Or Jung's.

L.P.   *What do you mean by complexity?*

J.H.   Freud was an extraordinary writer because of the complexity of the different things going on at the same time in his essays—he's pretending a case study in a medical sense; he's pretending to do cinema verité, what's actually happened; he's pretending to do a theoretical contribution to the nature of man, a piece of anthropology; and at the same time he's doing a very elaborate fiction, a very elaborate construction—and not without a little bit of pornography. But all of that makes his writing fascinating, and it appeals to many parts of the psyche. His case writings aren't just medical cases, and his theoretical writings aren't just theories. Besides, he isn't at all embarrassed about his fantasies: fantasies about Leonardo, about the primal horde, about death, or his fantasies about the little child's fantasies about sexuality or his fantasies about women . . . he puts it all in. And that complexity seems to me crucial for good psychology.

L.P.   *Perhaps psychology should look like a good novel. . . .*

J.H.   Mmm, yes!

L.P.   *And what kind of rhetoric do you think Jung used, as opposed to Freud?*

J.H.   Well, they're both pretending that at one level they're doing science. Jung complicated his writings by his tremendous number of references, it's what he calls amplifications. Anything that he wrote swelled up beyond what he wrote. He also complicated it through erudition. Freud put very little erudition in his writings, but he had a more consequential, step-by-step mind. Jung generally allowed four, five paragraphs to go off the track. Jung's complications are also stylistic, but in a romantic mode; Freud tried to write in a classical mode. But they are both terribly complicated. What people want now, of course, is general simplistic psychology. But good psychology has complications: Laing's come in his paradoxical twisting. With Laing it isn't in the wealth of the material as in Jung, and it isn't in the levels of what's going on in the whole mind, as in Freud; it's more in the twists of the mind going on in words.

L.P. *And where are your complications?*

J.H. Mine? I already said there is a terrible tension between trying to be very clear and always trying to twist it. And that's only one tension. Another one is between expansion and contraction. I want to write real tight, *knapp.* I'd love to be laconic, lapidary. To write telling quotable fragments, and yet everything expands and flows and wants to go on. Gertrude Stein says writing wants to go on.

L.P. *You also seem to love footnotes. You follow Jung more than Freud with your use of erudition. You have been criticized for these footnotes—as if they were merely for display.*

J.H. Footnotes! I can spend a whole morning chasing down one tiny little thing, making sure of some reference, checking it again. But there is something in this possession about erudition that's . . . well, a piece of my faith, how I see psychology. I try to bring in as much—let's call it culture—as I can. The soul must have it. I have the feeling that if I can only bring in all these cultural references, it will revitalize culture itself, connect the old library things with today's mind and today's mind with the libraries. It's a cultural concern. I want to show that psychology isn't a brand new thing because the soul isn't a brand new thing.

L.P. *Isn't that a very American ambition? American scholars are so full of quotations, so busy making culture.*

J.H. Not American psychology: it's all here and now, body, altered states of consciousness, instant rebirth, shot out of the birth canal like out of a circus cannon, head first with a helmet on. Bang. Fresh. Now. Wow. No footnotes there! For me, that's just not psychology. Complexity—and erudition is one way of complicating things—you put a mirror up to the psyche, like you said of a novel. . . . The psyche is very, very rich. Your own psyche is a mess of complexes and emotions and ideas, memories . . . if you can get as much of that into a piece, you're speaking to as much of the psyche as possible.

L.P.   *What actually goes on in your mind, in your fantasy, when you are writing? How does a book like Re-Visioning Psychology, such a massive and complicated book, take form?*

J.H.   When I was trying to finish the book, I was drawing battle maps. Every day, I drew a map of some section of the front to close off—say, between pages 81 and 85 or 112 to 113. And I had these gaps in the lines. I played the game of trying to fortify and seal whatever pages were still weak. I didn't write consecutively; I wrote different pieces at different weak spots of the front. This was the only way I could get done. Otherwise it became literal work, plugging ahead, page by page.

I remember writing "Abandoning the Child" in 1971 for an Eranos lecture. My image of it was a collection of very simple water colors. And I just wanted to do a little one here, one there, a little one on the "dead child," a little one on the "tree and child"... like you go through a gallery, and it didn't matter which picture came first; there was no conscious order between the phenomenological images of the theme. I didn't want to build anything, get heavy with it. I wanted to keep it all a series of images touched lightly, water colors. I gave that lecture and left afterward thinking it was an utter failure. (I often have that feeling anyway. An utter failure.) I felt the mode—the rhetorical style didn't work. It seemed too soft. Or my thinking was weak. I said to myself, now there you screwed up because of that aesthetic water-color fantasy. I attacked my fantasy of the form—not the ideas. Actually, the essay has since worked very well as a written piece. It's been taught and translated and photocopied and so on. But when I delivered it, it felt awful.

L.P.   *That was 1971 at Eranos. In 1968 your paper was on psychiatric language. It became the middle part of* The Myth of Analysis. *There the fantasy must have been altogether different since ...*

J.H.   Oh, Jesus, yes: that was a tremendous encyclopediac work. Collecting all those facts. I worked for months on that! Reading everything I could—medical history—to get new images of psychopathology. I had no particular physical fantasy like a battle or water colors. It was an encyclopedic kind of thing. When I worked on Dionysus and Hysteria [*Myth of Analysis,* part 3 (1969)], I remember saying I feel like I'm inside one of those great big sculptures, a Henry Moore, or one of those huge things of steel girders, and I'm doing all I can to weld huge chunks of steel together. It was like a great physical, exhausting, sculptural work. So those images of what I'm doing *when* I'm writing have nothing to do with *what* I'm writing, but they become necessary for my imagination to do it. It's like it prevents and it forms.

L.P.   *They're the "houses" of your writing (Heidegger, I believe).*

J.H.   The houses? They're the form. And they prevent me in some way or another from taking literally the essay as essay. They're saving graces. And they're like conductors because they remind me of music, of coming back to the same theme again. These fantasies just happen. I don't deliberately use them. I didn't think, "Now what is my image for this essay? Oh, it's a sculpture." It doesn't work like that. I'd get in my room and start typing . . . it was up in Sweden . . . in the summer. My first wife was Swedish, and we went there every year with our children, an island, and all that. And I would work on those long Eranos papers, and while I was sitting in a little white room working on those papers, I'd have that sense of being physically enveloped by the material I was working with—and that sculptural thing would embrace me, or the water colors.

L.P.   *We come back again to the physical . . .*

J.H.   . . . alchemical. It has to do with pressure. In that little room, I was building a head of steam. Unless the work builds a tremendous heat, I can't get at what I'm really working on, why I'm even writing it at all. But that heat keeps one from writing fluent cool prose. Ahh—the silver age of Latin. There's the Mediterranean fantasy again. Classical sentences. For me, it's more sulphuric, as if writing were a way of sublimating sulphur—so many hatreds boiling up, ideas to attack. Sulphur is the combustible element. It makes heat and expansion and so it needs condensing, and that means, shortening, tightening, skipping the little words and phrases that would make everything more understandable. The condensing makes the style dense, and that just builds more pressure and heat. It's a real alchemical circle.

L.P. *If your physical body carries this alchemical heat, I would guess that symptoms, what you call pathologizing, would have to accompany the process of writing.*

J.H. Not really—well, the shoulders get tight, and the face does too, around the eyes, they twitch if you are straining to "see." And the stomach . . . I've had ulcers . . . but not from writing. The hands do it mostly, with the stomach, and they enjoy it! I eat all the time when I'm working. But when I'm cutting trees in Sweden or swimming or walking around ruins for miles, I eat much less. It's the mind that needs good meals. We build body in writing: it's body-building. So, you may be working with "mere" words and just the tips of your fingers, but you actually create a *corpus,* a body, which becomes a person of its own, who is not "James Hillman"—but *that* we already talked about. Then, too, there is a wrestling match, a physical contest going on between the author's own physical body and the body of the work. So people who write sometimes say, "Boy, that book nearly killed me. It had me on the mat."

L.P. *Finger tips: that means you type your books.*

J.H. I type and I use scissors and paste and I run around my room looking things up. I have books and papers and notes. A huge table and everything all over the place. As soon as I've begun to work on something I make a mess of it . . . and more and more disorder and more and more activity making order out of it. But the physical activity is a joy and so is the disorder. I drink tea . . . I go downstairs and make a new cup of tea and forget to take the old cup down so there are tea cups all around, on top of everything else, but with all this disorder my mind is placed in the room, laid out there on the table, and that's why I can't clean the room up until the work is over. To lose a piece of it would be losing my mind.

10 WORKING

L.P. *Let's talk about therapy from the point of view of work.*

J.H. We'll have to start then from what therapy is all about. Therapy is not about consciousness; it is not even about self-development and, of course, it's not a medical treatment. What is it then? Is it basically to promote what the Jungians call "individuation"? I think not—or at least not as individuation is usually conceived. That idea needs to be rethought, not so much a process toward self-realization, like the completion of a destiny; individuation seems to me to be a necessary fantasy to carry one's hopes so that one can live one's oddity, realize one's individuality as wholly, as completely as possible at any moment. Now, that would mean that therapy is about being able to live, love, eat, think, do, respond—and work. So that therapy aims at bringing a person back to an unreflected way of working, an instinctual way of working. It's a crazy thing because the whole procedure is insight and reflection and conversation in an armchair, yet the intention is unreflected responsiveness, just plain old working—the mind working, the body working, the heart working, all by themselves without neurotic encumbrances. You know Freud said the whole business of therapy was to bring a person to love and to work. It seems to me we have forgotten half of what he said. Work. We have been talking of what goes wrong with love for eighty years. But what about what goes wrong with work? Where has that ever been discussed?

L.P. *But the notion of adaptive therapy, reeducation . . .*

J.H. Of course, these things have been taken into account, but let's not pretend they have been dealt with. You don't adapt people to the work: you adapt work to the people. I realize I am touching a delicate spot here. Work as *the* problem of human life is what Marxism has always been concerned with, but I'm not trying that kind of approach, because I question it. I question the Marxist economic idea of work, though they are right in insisting that work is primary. Work is what most of the people on this planet do: get up in the morning and go to work. Where do we learn to work, how do we learn to get the neurosis out of work, so that it *works* by itself, and what is the work instinct? We talk about the sex instinct, we talk about the eating instinct, or the aggressive instinct: what is the work instinct? I think there is a work instinct; it's what developed human civilization, and I think that this instinct in itself can be disturbed, affected, pathologized. . . . Like love and sex, work can have its pathologies.

L.P. *You mean that work no longer corresponds to money or that people do not work enough or that they don't know why they work and that work alienates people. . . .*

J.H. I do not mean pathologies in the economic sense. These things are all there, but this is not what I am trying to say. Let's take my kind of work, desk work. I sit down, and I am not working immediately with my hands when I stop and reflect: what shall I do? and what to do now? and what's going on? But when I pick something up, I start working; when I separate this paper from that paper, I move that book over there, I turn to the red pencil on the table that I am looking for, then I am working.

L.P. *This has rather dangerous implications. First it implies that when you are questioning "what to do now" you are not working, and second it implies that mental activities are not work, that only physical actions are work. Then, also, it implies that physical actions are "clean"—simple, good and not neurotic—but that questioning yourself is neurotic.*

J.H. Questioning in the right time and the right way is, of course, working. But questioning *instead* of letting your hands begin is not what your body sat you down at the table for. If you are at the work table, then you are where work happens. It's not fitting to question there as a defense against the hands. If questioning is the actual work now, then go take a walk or lie down and mull.

L.P.   *There is something wrong here: the example of you at your table implies that only physical actions of the hands are work.*

J.H.   The fault here, the problem here, is imagining the hands as mindless, as only physical. That's where the whole problem of work begins: right there in undervaluing and misapprehending the hands. Then work has to become an "ethic": you have to tell yourself to work, discipline children to work, reward people for their work. We moralize work and make it a problem, forgetting that the hands *love* to work and that in the hands is the mind. That "work ethic" idea does more to impede working . . . it makes it a duty instead of a pleasure. We need to talk of the work instinct, not the work ethic, and instead of putting work with the superego we need to imagine it as an id activity, like a fermentation, something going on instinctively, autonomously, like beer works, like bread works. Of course, that's ideal, as any instinct-theory of a human function tends toward idealism—instinct-theory tends to have Rousseau in it. Because right in the middle of working, I can lose my concentration. I am under attack. I can't do it or it seems boring, and I think, This is trivial, what I'm doing, this isn't important, I should be doing something much more important than this—that's one of the thoughts I have. What saves me right at this point is feeling that *everything* is important.

I have a fantasy, for example, that I have a farm, and it doesn't matter whether I'm correcting proofs or writing footnotes or reading some tiresome paper or other or editing somebody else's work . . . whatever I am doing, it's like a farm, and I have to feed the chickens and hoe the potatoes and chop the wood and do the accounts and pull the weeds. And every one of those jobs is necessary, and none is more important than the other one. So the new white page, the important new thought you are developing is not more important than the many little things that happen to be in your way or along your way. But they also happen to be the way itself. I don't have a monocentric image of work as if each person had one special task. If I ask myself, What's your task in life? I'm going to get a single answer. Questions like this come out of the ego so they only can have one answer—or a choice among single answers. Ego questions are set-ups—you can never answer them psychologically, with a polytheistic answer. So there isn't just one special task, like a calling or vocation. Vocation is a very inflating spiritual idea. One to one. God to me. Notice how our idea of Renaissance man is a polytheistic fantasy. He does all kinds of things. But vocation addresses the ego and makes it a specialist—then you "believe in yourself"—and that's another trap of that Devil, Belief—because who is believing in whom? I am believing in myself—all ego, and then I have a mission. Now that fantasy of the farm is polytheistic, and who is to say what is *the* important thing on a farm: the man who buys eggs from me would like more eggs and sees the time I spend chopping wood a waste. "Have a secretary do it. You have the best eggs around. Produce more, and even better ones." Specialization: the best eggman around; and that's monotheism and mission and early death! If you don't like the farm, then take a painter fantasy: a painter can be painting an oil or two of them and be reworking a piece he did twenty years ago and devising some new stain or mixture and be negotiating about a commission he has been offered and he does all these things at the same time.

L.P. *You seem to blur over a basic distinction that I learned myself in Switzerland—the distinction between Hauptsache and Nebensache, how to concentrate on main things and put off subsidiary, lesser things. One of the criticisms of a prime minister or a president is often that he pays too much attention to details at the expense of major policy, or vice versa. On your "farm" there seem to be no major tasks and no minor ones.*

J.H. My farm is a *psychological* fantasy, and therefore it tends to distribute the value into the actual tasks rather than having a *spiritual* farm where the tasks would be laid out in a hierarchy. "Importance" on my farm is not some overarching idea of a great canvas or a thousand-page history of psychology; importance appears in the way you do each thing. *Nebensache* becomes *Hauptsache* in how you do the work. It's very much like the old ends-means question, isn't it? The ends have to show their value in the very means you are using to gain the ends. Analysis is the perfect example: when you are working analytically, whatever the goal of analysis, the big ideas—consciousness, sensitivity, imagination, wholeness—have to be present in each reaction; those ends have to be right there in the work every little hour. I could put the same thing in military language: the strategy is right there in the tactics.

L.P. *That can be all right with intellectual work, but what about other kinds of work, repair work, house work, routine work, working in a factory or in the fields or driving a truck or work in the chemical industry where one gets poisoned by work....*

J.H. I can't talk about driving a truck, I don't know anything about it. Secretarial work . . . sometimes I type the same page four or five times....

L.P. *But that's your own writing!*

J.H. All right; what about a woman who walks into an office and types eight hours a day? What's wrong with that? Because there *is* something wrong. We are seeing it from a monotheistic perspective again—that person is not on a farm, that person has a specialty job. Specialty jobs are killing: you only do one thing. But if the person who sits at the typewriter all day also makes the coffee, also chooses the stationery and the furniture, also has to take care of that part of the office, clean the windows of that office, also has to go out and get the supplies of the office, shopping for the office, has to repair the typewriter, know something about her tools, then the whole thing changes, because it is just as important to keep the typewriter repaired and the window cleaned and maybe read something in connection with what she is typing: then it's no longer a specialty job, just being attached to the machine . . .

L.P. *But that is not what you are requested to do!*

J.H. No, that's not what you are requested to do because of that monotheistic style of work. Specialization has become serving only one God. So the woman doesn't have her empire, doesn't have her territory: a territory requires doing at least ten to fifteen things to be one's territory. Little altars everywhere. Instead she gets absolutely identified within an office with her job-description, her label. She won't even touch something different: "I don't get the supplies, they're supposed to be delivered by someone else to my desk"; "I don't make the coffee, I am better than making the coffee, that's done by the go-fer," "I don't run out to mail the letter." Actual life would be to go out and mail the letters, to go to the post office, to see other faces. And then you have a small empire, an entire territory, and you are back on the farm again, taking care of all its parts.

L.P. *You've still kept that secretary from the decision-making process. You've expanded her territory—but not into the boardroom. She remains a worker, even if less specialized.*

J.H. This emphasis on the "decision-making process" wouldn't be so strong if one were less specialized. The specialization makes one feel powerless—everything happens to me from outside except the one single thing I control. So I want to get in on the decision-making process. But if I can have a lot to say about my actual territory—its times, its style, its things, even its business forms (not the purchasing person only), and the people I work with (not the personnel office only), I am already in the decision-making process where that process actually is affecting my daily working.

L.P. *This is real utopia: it's certainly not the way society is structured!*

J.H. Is it really so difficult to make those very small changes? Can't we reclaim more of our jobs; try to own it all? The more you take in, the more the farm increases and broadens out; everything belongs. The specialist, monotheist view of work is really dreadful. It assumes people don't want to work and that they prefer to have as little to do as possible, just one single job. But in fact, there is a natural *Triebsamkeit,* an activity connatural with human being. You wake up in the morning, and even if you are depressed eventually you want to be doing something. A disaster strikes, a flood or avalanche, and the first thing that happens, once the immediate ruin and horror is tended to, is people cleaning and sweeping and putting things in order and working double time. We want desperately to work, and unemployment is a terrible disease to endure. But unemployment is not just when there are no jobs. It goes on in the fantasy of work that now dominates us: specialization is a kind of unemployment because we are not fully working, not employing our fullness.

L.P. *To develop this idea of work as instinctual, you would have to relate it more tightly with patterns of behavior and with symptoms, the disturbances in behavior, so that it becomes more evident that work reflects id more than superego.*

J.H. Well, let's take depression again—that favorite topic of this interview—it is classified mainly as a mood disorder. Subjectivism. But how in fact do we recognize depression first of all? How does it present itself? People say, at least in Switzerland, "I just couldn't get up, I couldn't go to work." It appears first as a *work* disorder. The subjectivism: fears of sickness and poverty, sadness and black mood—they could all be seen partly as results of not working. The instinct to work is not functioning. And, it is interesting, that the main therapy—again in Switzerland at Burghölzli when I learned there, is work therapy. Not occupational merely to keep occupied, but real work on the farm and mechanical shop. You can see compulsion also as a work disorder. Workaholics; obsession; can't stop. Even some Freudian defense mechanisms are first of all, or appear first of all, as work disorders. Undoing, for instance; or reaction formation—where a person's whole notion of work and style of working is to keep everything else at bay.

L.P. *By returning work to an instinct theory, you want to remove its problems to the psychological field and away from the social, political, and economic fields.*

J.H. That's a bit too ambitious: I merely want to speak of working as a *pleasure,* as an instinctual gratification—not just the "right to work," or work as an economic necessity or a social duty or a moral penance laid onto Adam after leaving Paradise. The hands themselves *want* to do things, and the mind loves to apply itself. Work is irreducible. We don't work for food-gathering or tribal power and conquest or to buy a new car and so on and so forth. Working is its own end and brings its own joy; but one has to have a fantasy so that work can go on, and the fantasies we now have about it—economic and sociological—keep it from going on, so we have a huge problem of productivity and quality in our Western work. We have got work where we don't want it. We don't want to work. It's like not wanting to eat or to make love. It's an instinctual laming. And this is psychology's fault: it doesn't attend to the work instinct.

L.P. *When you are supposed to be working a certain number of hours, you get into a certain kind of time, entirely different from the time "outside" work. That is another kind of time. Even if you are not working on a line in a factory, there is always a kind of time you build in as you are working, a time that is "in" the work.*

J.H. You are so right! Working time is time *in* the job, not just on the job. The work dictates to you the style of that time; whether this is to be done quickly or slowly, or to be repeated or to be done without noticing what you are doing, as if you do it only by your hands. I wouldn't call that mechanically, I would call that instinctively, manually. It's in the hands. The sense of tiredness governs, the dynamic feeling rather than the clock determines it. It's your body that determines the work, the rhythm to pace yourself. If you start moving too quickly, you can feel yourself being burnt out: it's getting too hot, you are working too fast. I work so quickly with paper sometimes that my hands are out of control, one hand hurts the other hand, like people in the kitchen when they cut themselves, burn themselves. Their hands have lost connection with the body and with the work; they're moving faster than the work. The hands govern the work— or maybe the work paces the hands. And when it's slow—like the first few days of beginning something, it's terribly slow, slow energies as they say, cold mutton, you put something aside or you see a patient you have not seen for so many weeks or years . . . to get things going again takes so much time. That's determined by the nature of the work, the matter of the work, not by the clock and not by the money.

L.P. *So this could be a way of coming back to one of Jung's ideas, the idea of "opus"?*

J.H. But here we have to watch out. Opus is tied to individuation—a kind of single-tracked thing, going forward, or filling out. It is a "becoming" fantasy: the opus of oneself, one's self-realization, or the self's realization. Instead, let's tie opus to crafting, making something. That's what *poesis* means: making. So when I speak of soul making, I am imagining the opus of the soul as a work that is like a craft, and the models for it would come from the arts. . . .

L.P. *The arts provide visible analogies for the invisible work, as you said in one of your lectures, the one in Florence.*

J.H. Also the artists. The opus is not only the product, it's *how* they work. Isn't it curious how little we know about *how* they work?

L.P. *Well, we do know they work with their hands, and you keep mentioning hands. . . .*

J.H. And where do their hands learn how to work? They learn from the tools they work with and from the materials. The hammer teaches you how to hold it so you can hit the nail and the wood teaches you how hard you have to hit, whether it's soft or a piece of very hard walnut. Psychology doesn't recognize this. Psychology still thinks that the material world is dead so how can it teach you anything. Psychology still tells you that tools are an extension of the hand, part of the ego, instruments of willpower. Invented for problem solving. But the hand doesn't use tools, tools use the hand and teach it how to work. So to begin with, we learn about working by noticing more in detail how we actually go about working. It's amazing how little we can find out about working itself. Go to a bookstore and you'll find books on how to make love in a hundred positions, how to cook anything—soups, beans—whole books just on cooking beans: but no instruction at all on the sensitivity, the rhythm, the psychological and physical details of working: how to govern your concentration, your speed, your inflation, your energy and attention, how and when to stop, what else to do. How to deal with the sense of being stupid or helpless or inferior or doing it wrong. . . .

L.P. *There are many books about success and getting ahead and improving your concentration. . . .*

J.H. True, but I am reaching here for something else—it's not a program or rules. It's what one goes to a teacher for, what a painter goes to another painter for—not just how he handles the materials, but to watch his rhythm, what he does first, how he eats when he works . . . all kinds of little things. How he sits in the saddle. When you go to school now, academic schools, you learn material, you learn stuff; do you ever see a professor working? He works at home. You don't know what the hell he does at home when he comes in with the lecture or he sits for the seminars; you don't see him *at work.* You don't see his relationship with his body or his milieu in the process of working. To go into a professor's study would be the way you should learn to work, to spend the whole day with him. I went to see Kerényi once, and I remember seeing him at his table. He was reediting one of his older essays, and he had pasted onto the printed pages of the early edition hundreds of little slips of new footnotes, new sentences, new little pieces, it was a giant mass of little corrections, of detailed fancy work, fancy in the sense of intricate: that is to see how to work. You don't see it when you buy his book; it's all hidden. You don't know anything about the actual *poesis,* the making of the opus. And it's this art of the work that seems to me what you ought to be trained to do. When analysts meet each other or writers, they often ask how many hours do you work? When? How do you arrange your day? Where do you work? They talk about eating in relation with work or about getting tired, about many small details of the act of working. They don't mainly ask about fees or ideas or whether a book is selling or not. Curiosity is about the activity of working itself. Our sexual curiosity is being taken care of more and more in the movies, but we don't see enough precision of working.

L.P. *Your idea of work may be a farm fantasy, but you really are speaking of work in an aesthetic way. It's not labor, it's not drudgery, it's not working for someone else . . .*

J.H. Sometimes that can be easier. Have you any idea what the demon demands! He doesn't give you a single day off and no fringe benefits, and there is no union that can call him off your back. But you are right: we have to re-vision work in an aesthetic way and get it out of the all-too-economical Marxist view of it as drudgery, the alienation of man in work. Psychoanalysis has neglected work, so it all remained in the Marxist scenario. But I don't want to go into that. I can't really. You know more about that in Italy. All I actually know is my work and my way of working.

L.P. *It is astounding to me, from a culture that has had such a long Marxist influence, that you can speak of working quite separated from economics.*

J.H. We have to make that move because that link between work and money is precisely what makes us feel like slaves. Arise: you have nothing to lose but your chains; but the chains are that linkage between money and work. If we could just loosen that linkage, work could be returned to instinct and it could be reimagined as a psychological phenomena, a soul activity, not an economic activity, merely. Patients, people, are desperately looking for work that really *pays*—work that gives them credit, that has interest and value, that gives them shares. Money-pay is a substitute for these soul needs. The language of economics has usurped all the soul terms for richness and worth—value, interest, credit, trust, assets, bonds, and so forth and so on, and so work can't get free of money without losing the language and feeling of worth. It's very much like love that has become chained to sex, so work has become chained to pay.

L.P. *I don't believe you are saying that money and sex are evil, are you? You are not now taking an ascetic, Catholic position against Marxism, are you?*

J.H. Goodness no! I'm trying to say that the instinct to work like the instinct to love has got confused with part of the act, the gratification of being paid, rewarded, or the gratification in sexual pleasures. Just as love is satisfying in itself, so is work satisfying. We must not define an instinctual activity with one part or phase of it. Psychology still talks about rewards as things that happen at the end of an activity, rather than happening within the functioning of the activity. Psychology calls this "positive reinforcement," as if positive feelings weren't reinforcing the instinctual activity all along the way. That's how an instinct feels. It likes what it is doing. It has its own goal, for that's the nature, the definition, of instinct. That is, unless you ask it to do something in an uninstinctual setting like a psychologist's lab where the rewards are separated from the activity. But it is disastrous to separate out satisfactions, the final cause or goal of an action, from the functioning of it. Then the functioning becomes meaningless in itself and one hurries toward the payoff. The payoff is a displacement: you defend yourself against the joy of work, letting go in it, the libidinal id passion of it by high pay, more money—and, of course, it is never enough and you feel bought or obligated. That ruins work and ruins love. If earning money is the aim of work, or even if the ideal of the community is the aim of work, this devalues the work, and someone who just loves working is called a "workaholic" or whatever. And one concentrates on the payoff, the money, all the ways to spend it—the consumer society—instead of concentrating on differentiating the instinct of working. But all this has been analyzed far more competently....

Though I do want to say one thing about leisure—the old classical idea of *otium*. It has been corrupted by the senex. In America they speak of the work ethic as if work is tied only to the reality principle: hard work, hard labor, hard reality, and hard money, too. Real things, good things, are always *hard*. Never mind the sexual implications, now, just notice how puritanism and capitalism like these hard words. I have patients who simply cannot work in that senex way. They get paralyzed when work is split off from pleasure. Now, as this puritan ethic and its monotheistic notion of God breaks down—God, the eternal Overseer—of course, work gets free of the senex work ethic, and so leisure might now be freeing itself from the puer. Leisure has been caught up by childish puer fantasies of silly games, wasted time, fantasy vacations, flights. Cocaine as the ultimate puer trip after a hard day's work. We need the old idea of *otium* again because that was a cultivated, an educated leisure, an anima leisure for the soul, not a puer leisure to escape a moral monotheistic Marxist senex notion of work. In America, for instance, we have achieved for many, many people the ideal of the Marxist society—or at least the ideal put forth by Marx's disciple Lassalle, leisure. We have lots of leisure, but no education for it at all. Leisure without soul. We have a leisure class utterly caught in puer kinds of rewards because of the senex notion of work. If senex earns, puer spends; if senex works, puer plays, and so on . . .

L.P. *There are particular feelings attached to work. For instance when you get stuck or repetitive because what you are doing is boring you feel you can't cope with it or you are not really up to it. But those feelings are part of the work, just as the positive aspects of it (you would probably call them inflated): the excitement when you get to something, when you are having a new idea and you feel you are doing something, really flowing and complete. How do all these different feelings belong to the work?*

J.H. The belong to the *ritus* of the work. They're not personal feelings: everyone has them. Work is ritual, and part of the ritual is waste, repetition, boredom, the sense of this-is-a-whole-morning-wasted: I spent three hours in the library, four hours, and I started reading other things that have nothing to do with what I am working on. I have a deadline on Saturday, and I wasted this whole Wednesday morning, it's insane. This is one kind of despair. Another despair: you can't get the thought and it comes in a lump, and no matter how hard you try to write the same paragraph, you can't get the thing to come out. Then you have to leave it in that lump. Another kind of despair is: you don't any longer know what you are saying, what you are doing. You've lost somehow what it is all about. Those senses of inferiority, of waste, of being blocked, of being unable, as you said, are tremendously important, because in the psyche there is a reason for the block.

Maybe the psyche needs to stay longer where it is, in the dark or as a lump. The feelings of inferiority are also part of the work in another sense: they counteract the fiction of perfection that is necessary for the work to be conceived in the first place. How can you begin anything without a fiction of perfection—that this is going to be the best! That fiction is part of the impetus. Someone said the only joy in work is beginning it, conceiving it . . . another puer fantasy, of course, and not one I wholly subscribe to, since I love the anal moment of ending, executing, closing off and sending the work to the typist for "fresh, clean copy" and a pat on the head, a smile. But anyway, the fantasy of perfection inevitably carries with it the fantasy of imperfection and failure. Inferiority. These two fantasies go on together, almost simultaneously—and they must. If they get split apart, one goes through manic-depressive cycles in working. When they are together, and not in up-or-down phases, one lives both the puer enjoyment *and* the senex criticism. Puer is not merely content, you know, and not even only the style. Puer shows most in the energy, the blind enthusiasm that makes for a sureness that can become a literalism. When you work in and through the Puer, you are always "up"—even if the content is about nuclear catastrophe. It's like working with an erection. It is silly to hold that puer people are lamed and weak and unable to work: often they are almost psychopathic in their energy for working.

L.P. *Psychopathic?*

J.H. Because they have lost the soul to the energy. They don't know what they are doing anymore, or why; there is so much joy in the activity itself. It lets them fly. Now Marx didn't know much about puer working. Marx was a monotheist: one fantasy of work, only, and literal, economic. The puer attitude in work never imagines itself as part of a class, a proletariat. Even if a person is a cook in a fast-food place or scraping paint—that is, doing lowly "labor," feeling abused and underpaid, still the puer energy floats him above the job into a feeling of his own specialness. His reality is not what Marx or Freud would call reality. His solidarity is with the Divine Flow not with human suffering—unless, of course, the human suffering has become a vision itself which, of course, again loses touch with actual human suffering. . . .

But I want to go back to those two fictions—perfection and inferiority or failure—that go with intellectual work. I want to stress that the bottom aspect, the failure, the inferiority feeling, as Alfred Adler showed, is just as important psychologically when you are working as is the top aspect: the ambition, the sense of power, the hope, or what Adler called the "striving for perfection." That striving for perfection is part of the process of every human activity, but we should not make the psychological mistake of identifying it with the whole process which absolutely requires stubborn blocks, inferiorities, impasses. My own habit is never to push those places: if something doesn't work on page 31, I go to page 46, I go wherever there is movement. I let my sense of weakness guide me, not my striving for perfection only. I never try to reduce something that is stubborn, directly; I give up on it and then come back and try again. Let's take it as a military action: I don't try to reduce cities that have a strong resistance; I move through to wherever else it goes. And "to wherever else it goes" can be to go down and do the dishes or can be to retype pages that I did before or can be to chase down something that I said somewhere and that I have lost for I moved too quickly: I have to go back and pick it up again. So there's always something to do on the farm, or on the battlefield, even if I am not up to attacking the main problem. The work goes on working anyway, and there comes into your head exactly what you were trying to get at: then you make a note for yourself, put it on the table, and the next day you can work with it.

L.P. *Would you say that your analytical work also follows this method of never reducing strong resistances, of always following the movement?*

J.H. Analytical work is tricky because the movement may actually be concealed right there where it seems resistant and blocked. (My wife wrote a paper on that, too: "Stopping as a Mode of Animation.") Sometimes it's more like laying siege—not direct attack on a resistance, but pretty well surrounding it, walking around and around it, reinforcing it almost, so that the resistance feels itself utterly self-enclosed, really blocked. Then the gates may just open. Analytical work needs hundreds of different fantasies—not techniques, not methods—but fantasies within which one can work. It can be baseball or bullfighting or cooking or farming or military strategy or weaving or shell collecting or sculpting. . . . Unless you have a fantasy of work, there is only work as collectively conceived, a kind of literalism that is either Marxist or psychoanalytic "working through"—very heavy, very dull, very resentment producing. One needs a fantasy that gives a body feeling, a manual feeling to the job you are engaged in. And it helps in therapy to mention casually along the way which fantasy you are working with, because one of the things therapy has to do is to work on the problem of work itself in the patient, help the patient learn in therapy how to imagine the act of working. So, if I can say what fantasy we are in now: encircling the city of high walls or turning up the heat a little or trying to get more rose-madder and aquamarine and naples yellow into the picture, then these fantasies keep the analytical work from becoming literalized into a "what-we-are-supposed-to-be-doing," some abstract concept, some idol called "analysis."

L.P. *You said at a certain point that this art of the work, this crafting, seemed to you what one ought to be trained to do. You used examples of painters watching painters or yourself editing in collaboration. Well, now isn't this what training analysis is?*

J.H. Oh, I've always joked that editing is therapy because it makes both parties very, very intensely conscious of the minutiae of style, of the shadow in the ways of the mind, that is, how the unconscious mind works. A training analysis has to be like editing, otherwise it's just copying silence! If the analyst simply sits there—suppressing—then all you learn is suppression. What one wants to learn in training of any kind is tiny little moves, how the "master" actually works—how to make the shots in sports, or, well, how exactly to cook those beans. And a recipe won't do it, and practice may not either: you have to watch that chef . . . how he moves his hands, where he puts his feet. You have to get into his kitchen.

11 LOVING

L.P. *You once said that love in therapy is more important than consciousness, and that you were hanged on that sentence. But what is love in therapy for you?*

J.H. Love is one word for so many different phenomena, but in all of them ... well, isn't love so very literal, so concrete? The question is, What's the psyche doing by making us fall into this concrete desire, this desire for the concrete, that we fall into in most kinds of love? Because you do fall, you do fall in. A *Fall* in German is a trap, and it is also a case, just like the Latin *cadere* which means to fall and is the root of the word "case." The moment you are in love you are a case. You've fallen into a trap, the trap of concrete desire, like a trapped animal. Caught. But, we haven't fallen into sin. We haven't fallen into "animal desire." What's happened is that we are now suddenly conscious of the cage we have placed around the animal, and so we blame the animal and say we have fallen into the animal. But the animal doesn't *fall* in love; he doesn't have to—not because he is already fallen, but because he doesn't start off with an ego that believes it isn't an animal, and then has to fall.

L.P. *"The moment you are in love you are a case." ... Could you say more about this neurotic or pathological aspect of love?*

J.H. The sense of being bewitched or transfigured or whatever, belongs to being in love because love is one of the forms in which the normal ego has to submit to the psyche, as it does in depression, as it does in ambition. The ego becomes possessed, taken over by psyche. So, to regard a state of love as a salvation or as a delusion, either way doesn't give the love itself much. What is the love doing; what does the psyche want in this love? Love isn't only the endless description of your feeling and the discovery of the subjective world. Certainly it can also be that nuancing of subjectivity—and, of course, it makes you more attentive, more sensitive. But love is mostly an explosion of imagination, an extraordinarily powerful way the psyche produces its images. We need to recognize this explosion of images and not let love turn into a mere subjectivism and revel in its feelings. We need to see through the usual, direct, psychotic sort of literalism that is hung up on the other person—I've got to hear your voice every two hours, phone me, or, I've got to get my hands on you, or, I drive past your door in the middle of the night—obsession. What is the psyche doing in this psychotic sort of attachment? Evidently I need, or the psyche needs, a concrete other person. But why does the psyche make love so obsessively concrete, and why do all the disciplines of loving from Plato to transference emphasize moving beyond the concrete? The other person has become a mysterious incendiary, some kind of fuse that ignites the imagination *concretely,* makes the imagination terribly, passionately real, physical, alive, desirable. That's what I must have meant when I said love was more important than consciousness, because love forces the imagination on you as *the* reality. Lovers are always looking for the reason why they fell in love with each other. They tell tale after tale about it, in order to make the crazy mystery of it endurable. (Transference is one of those "tales.") But it becomes endurable only by realizing that love is *the* necessity of the psyche in its struggle with the concrete—for some to get more into the concrete, for others to find a way through it, but always love involves the psyche in the mad impossibility of direct concrete physicality.

L.P.   *If transference love is one of those tales, are you saying that transference is a fiction? Are you saying that transference is a way of drawing the two persons into the tales of love?*

J.H.   I think what I'm saying is that transference is the struggle with the fall into psychotic concretism. Of course, analysts get caught by erotic transference and countertransference: their job, our job, is eroticizing imagination. Now what is that? I just mean getting the sensual sexual reality of images. The saints knew all about that.

L.P.   *They lived in chastity. Does one have to deny the concrete flesh to "eroticize the imagination"?*

J.H.   These are awful questions because however you answer you will be wrong. Still, psychoanalysis, with its libido theory, with its idea that sex is *the* basic drive, puts analysts into a terrible dilemma. When sex appears in analysis, in transference feelings, one can't help but believe it is irreducible, hence literal—aha, now we are at the real root. The only reduction of these sexual feelings is to other ones, earlier ones, like incest. But the psyche never said sex was the real root—Freud said it. The psyche says *it* is the real root; *it* is basic, its images; so the job is reducing the sexual to the imaginal, seeing that the sexual is being used by the psyche as a push, a goad, a "drive," as it is called, forcing the concrete into psychic reality, forcing us to recognize that a concrete sexual obsession is not only sexual, not only what it claims it is, but that it is an activity of imagination.

L.P.   *And analysis becomes the place, maybe the one and only modern place, where this recognition of the psychic aspect of sexuality can happen. It does require chastity then, or what Freud called withholding?*

J.H.   No doubt about it, and all analysts know this and yet they are constantly "falling," falling all over the place, and sometimes they don't even feel it as a fall. Why?

L.P.   *Why?*

J.H.   Well . . . one of the delusions of love is that it is a salvation—and one of the signs that analysis is off the track, getting spiritual instead of psychological, is when sexuality gets spiritualized. Then sexuality becomes tantric and magical: you're falling but you believe you are going up. It feels like salvation, initiating the patients sexually for their own good. All the psychological problematics have fallen away: no inhibitions, no compulsions, no "fall," just bliss. Again, this is not a sexual problem, it is a spiritual one.

L.P.   *Even so, why doesn't the professional rule of chastity hold?*

J.H. The rule has to have the right location. It can't be just a medical rule or a legal rule because that locates it in the superego and what superego can hold out against a lovely luring id, sweet Maribelle grown up! So, we have to locate the rule of chastity *psychologically*, back it with an image. Then it can work like a container, a vessel, rather than a fence—a defense. Then the images of sexuality themselves become the containers of it. Then the indulgence in the images actually chastens them—in alchemy it's called whitening the sulphur—and the concretism becomes less compulsive. Enjoyment is already going on. It's not on the other side of the fence. But the horrible thing is that love always insists on breaking the rules. Eros is devious and wily and Venus is unprincipled and Pan is a nightmare force! And Dionysus—you know he is worshipped in the shape of a phallus. Analysis invites in terrible powers.

But these are the Gods of conjunction, what Freud called the unifying principle. For me, the interesting part of love is usually its decay, that is, the impossibility. When it falls apart, when it doesn't work, when all the pathologies appear (and aren't disguised in bliss). You see this decay in dreams when the old lovers don't want each other any more, when an old attraction, an old pattern doesn't work. And then you are haunted by them, the old figures, for years afterward. They return like ghosts. The eros is getting psychized. Then you have something very painful but very interesting to work with. What are these ghosts returning for?

L.P. *Love has so many miseries—the psychotic delusions, the obsessive memories, those ghosts, the hysteria, the narcissism. Psychoanalysis seems little different from nineteenth-century literature in its preoccupation with the pathologies of love.*

J.H. Oh, I think analysis is a big improvement over that literature. The novelists put first value on the emotions, exploring them, analyzing them. What I try to do is not to put the feelings first but the images, that is not to call something miserable because your feeling is miserable, but to examine the misery in terms of the image. That gives a new handle on it. What is the precise image of the misery? It may be yourself, chained, unable to move. Or yourself like Cinderella, sitting by the fire and deserted, or yourself thrown into a ditch or hated, paranoid, everybody laughing at you and betraying you. Or your misery may be screaming and calling and burning for the other person—in a particular place or scene. I remember once my own misery showed in a dream as a leopard that was on fire inside my bloodstream. You'd be amazed at the images that lie inside the feelings—but one thing is sure, there always will be some revelatory image. Once a woman patient was tortured by a lover who left her—and what was this torture, really, in her imagination? It was a tall erect phallus, and she was bowing, and it just stood there imperious, impervious, and she was groveling . . . now that was a revelatory image. And it gave her something to work with. When you see the image, then you can begin to see the archetypal structures and the myths that are going on in the various feelings you have, and then the feelings become a kind of necessary quality of the image, rather than being obsessive in themselves. The image gives you an imagination of the feeling. The image frees you from your obsession with feelings. As the images change, the feelings change. Unfortunately most psychology has been emphasizing feeling all the time and then reducing these feelings back to parental feelings or sexual feelings rather than imagining the feelings through in detail or mythologizing them. It can help to play your love against the rich background of suffering offered by myths, by literature and drama: then what's going on not only begins to make new sense, but also cultures you.

L.P. *But isn't there a narcissistic foundation to love; isn't that myth most important and the reason why love is always disappointing, maybe even delusional?*

J.H. Why call it narcissistic? Why mix up autoerotic subjectivism with one of the most important and powerful myths of the imagination—just think of how many writers and painters and poets have been drawn to Narcissus, and philosophers, including Plotinus. This confusion of Narcissus with narcissism kills a certain kind of love, the love for images. To enter imagination, to imagine at all, you have to desire the image itself—without any concern for what it comes from or that it might be an image *of* something else. The image is the reality. Narcissus leans out and over and into the image; he is not wrapped up in his own feelings, his own self. He has forgotten himself, subjectivism completely gone, no narcissism whatsoever! The image fills his consciousness and his desire. But the way "narcissism" is used in psychology is another rationalistic attack on imagination and on the myth itself which has tremendous profundities in it about reflection, about resonance and echo, about the physical passion for the image, devotion to the image, about beauty and death. . . . Narcissus gives his whole life over to an image. But psychology is terrified of Narcissus. It just will not allow anyone to love images wholeheartedly and take them for real. It just will not allow love to be imaginal.

The myth is extreme enough, dramatic enough, to be useful for pathology, but that does not mean that the myth is simply pathological. All the great mythical tales and figures are useful for envisioning our human pathologies, but to read them backward, to read from the human version of these pathologies a corresponding pathology in the myth is a humanistic distortion. Narcissus is not merely narcissistic. The term "narcissism" sees the love in the myth wholly from the secular normal view of mental health, missing the subtlety, the redemptive motif in the myth. If we could really get inside this figure we could see how love works in the imagining mind and how the psyche works within the subject: through images and love for them.

L.P. *If the imaginal method of working with love in therapy is an improvement over nineteenth-century literary modes of analyzing love, would you go on to say that therapy has had an improving effect on love, that analysis has made us either more imaginative or more realistic, or just "better" in regard to love?*

J.H. No. Probably, just the contrary. There is too much that psychoanalysis has ignored. We know all about transference love and incest love and mother love, and "the vicissitudes of the sexual instinct" as it's called. But literature knows lots of kinds of love: greed, love for money, gluttony, the love of country, the love of one's birthplace, of one's land. And the love for one's religion—that can be an immense and complicated kind of love. Or what about the love of justice. To sound very simple now: you can love a river. And what does psychoanalysis do with that? Make it a genital symbol or a life symbol, but there can be very deep emotion, enough to found a settlement, constellated by a river.

You see, psychoanalysis has narrowed love to what goes on between two people. But the love that goes on in a human soul in therapy may reflect concerns of that soul beyond incest, beyond even the Psyche-Eros myth, into other avenues of love altogether, extending right into the world. The treatment of eros in psychoanalysis has been too narrow. Even family love that was the first subject of early psychoanalysis is such a mystery and such a value that it can be destroyed by psychoanalysis. It's no use calling these attachments simply a "mother complex" or "sibling rivalry" . . . they are far too deep, too interesting. Jung's insight into kinship libido as the basis of transference and communal bonding was a big step in the right direction—but even this is too simple, too general, because the phenomena of love need to be explored each in its own way. The other fundamental mistake in psychoanalysis is the study of adult love in terms of babies and small children. We really do need a new critique of depth psychology in terms of what it has done to love in our century.

L.P. *What other aspects of love have been neglected by depth psychology?*

J.H. If we stay a moment with community, I think neither Jung's kinship libido nor Adler's *Gemeinschaftsgefühl,* or social feeling, go far enough, because the first community are the dead, the ancestors, the community of souls. This kind of love may be more basic to what goes on in analysis—its work with figures, its work with voices, with memories, and the mystery of analysis itself, the bonding it can create, and the mystery of your own death—than any of the other drives or ideas of love. We don't die alone. That's an ego view, a lonely isolated view. Death is communal, entering the community of the dead, and these dead are already present in the heart. I think they are there, like presences. They may be the ground of love. An underworld ground. I don't know. Who does? But love is grounded in something way beyond the ideas of the consulting room. Maybe love comes to us from the dead, from Gods. We think *we* do the loving, that it starts in our hearts, but what images are moving there that set love going—and in such strange ways, for such strange people and strange things? It's so archetypal that it makes us into living archetypes—and even years of analysis can't altogether straighten out, humanize, the demonic, archetypal things going on in love.

L.P. *You say that each of the archetypes has its own style of love, and that is why you wrote that we cannot place all love at a single altar, whether the altar of Venus or Eros or Jesus or the Great Mother—or the Underworld.*

J.H. Monotheism again. Do you see how it creeps in everywhere. But even monotheism, in the sense of Old Testament jealousy, is a style of loving. The senex too has its passions and loyalties. Loyalty can be the main way certain people exhibit their love. Those old eighteenth-century males, like Pope and Swift and Cavendish, loved mainly through loyalty. Many of them were bachelors, but they were loyal to their friends, their clubs, their associations, their political positions. Psychoanalysis has omitted friendship. . . .

L.P. *There is always a homosexual component in friendship. . . .*

J.H. You know, the very first psychological paper I wrote was "Friends and Enemies." It was not liked. The paper tried to show that friendship was more important than transference, that friendship was the classical virtue and the hardest achievement in a man's life from Aristotle through the Renaissance, and that there are many kinds of friendship which Thomas Aquinas lays out in detail . . . it tried to show that for real friendship there have to be real enemies who are not mere shadow projections to be "integrated."

L.P. *It sounds very antipsychological.*

J.H. Isn't that just the point? Psychology has got itself into a position where the major virtues and motifs of human life have become antipsychological. Let's say instead that psychology is anticultural. Even your question about friendship having a homosexual component shows this *deformation professionelle* of psychology.

L.P. *It depends on how you regard homosexuality. If you see it as a perversion or if you see it as a sexual, a Venusian moment, or an erotic moment, that engenders friendship.*

J.H. Oh! in that sense, of course, there is a homosexual component in friendship. A friend is someone you want to be physically close with—eating, fishing, sitting around. Doing things together. Even talking is a physical reality. Look at all the talking going on in the Socratic dialogues! Homosexuality has been reduced to men putting their penises through toilet walls—utterly impersonal pickups, autonomous genitals. Homosexuality is far more than this; it is homoerotics, the eros between, between men, between women, or between "likes"—similars, familiars, sames. Homoerotics has become confused with autoerotics, but autoerotics can appear in heterosexuality just as it does in homosexuality. . . .

There was an old Jungian analyst, a very remarkable man, John Layard, who gave me a great deal of love, of friendship, and he was always breaking down and looking for an analyst, especially among younger men because he claimed that Jung hadn't understood and wouldn't even try to understand homoeroticism. So he wanted to do some analysis with me—and I refused because I wanted to keep our relationship as a friendship. Again I valued love or friendship more than analytical consciousness. Our connection was working in the friendship archetype; it seemed wrong to shift to another archetypal pattern. There is a kind of collaboration of psyches that goes on in friendship—not necessarily that the friends actually work together on the same or similar projects but the psyches collaborate, affect each other, move each other. The friend enters your imagination and fertilizes it: that is some of the homosexuality in friendship. Men patients who are quite closed in on themselves are very resistant to the homosexual advances and attractions that appear in their dreams. Usually these images are interpreted as proof of latent homosexuality and therefore the patient's closedness is seen as a result of his latent homosexuality. But this has it backwards because the homosexual advances made to him by the psyche are precisely the healing that could open him up to taking in another spirit, being penetrated, opened. Homoeros can move you out of closedness; it doesn't have to make you more closed.

Friendships are so hard to maintain because they continually demand accessibility, that you let yourself take in the other person, let your imagination be stirred by thoughts, approaches, feelings that shake you out of your set ways. I am more angry and more intolerant—I mean I rage and shout more at my friends and with my friends than I do with anyone else. But this is only one tiny aspect of friendship. It is far more complicated than that—even the eros that moves through archetypal psychology, that we spoke of the other day, is a kind of communal friendship. All I want to get over is the value of these kinds of love—homoeros, friendship—and point up that the culture has always recognized their importance from the Greeks through the Renaissance and the romantic movements and that they are just not paid the right attention in psychology today.

L.P. *You were mentioning other aspects of love, less personal. Were you meaning mystical love or religious love, Western or Eastern, spiritual or physical?*

J.H. I was probably thinking of something much closer at hand. I meant love that is fixated to pairing, coupling, the dyad, the delusion of reciprocity, you call it. A third has to come in. Love itself makes this move. It brings in the triangle, and that's the importance of jealousy: it makes you awfully conscious of the third. Just look at this interview: the interview itself is a kind of love. It is moving the psyche back and forth as a third thing is being explored, the interview. It would not work if there were not a love going on as we work. And what is that love? Is it love for each other? We don't know each other. But there is a reciprocity somewhere, although it is not just between the two of us . . . there is a reciprocity in regard to what is happening. So it is the *interview*—not our relationship—the *object* of our love: a work, a forming, a making. You see, love is not a phenomenon of the person, love is a phenomenon of the spirit and it stirs the soul and generates imagination.

L.P. *And imagination always needs a third thing, like Narcissus' mirror. Love cannot happen without a third.*

J.H. Exactly. Imagination is the thing, and love cannot happen without the third, what Erik Erickson calls "generativity." The final stage of love for him is when it generates. Plato, too, called it generativity, and he connected that generativity with beauty, with the infinite power of imagination to form. How can one do an interview without love, without imagination working, without this attempt going on all the time as we sit here struggling to generate the interview itself into a form, making our work as true, as beautiful, as accurate, as well spoken as we possibly can. You see there is an idealism in our very working, what we called inflation early on, and that is eros right here.

L.P. *Must the third always be a product? Must the third be a child or a new state of the soul resulting from the two persons? I would think that the third isn't merely something produced by love but is the love itself, and is prior to the two persons.*

J.H. I have come to realize that the third is the problem, the difficulty, the pathology itself. Yes, it seems prior to the relationship and governs the relationship. Why do we focus so intensely on our problems? What draws us to them? Why are they so attractive? They have the magnet power of love: somehow we desire our problems; we are in love with them much as we want to get rid of them, and they seem there before a relationship begins, before an analysis begins. Now, if the problem contains some strange compelling fascinating third, then it is a love object or is a place where love itself is hiding, right in the problem. This means that problems are secret blessings or, let's say, they are not so much problems as they are emblems—like Renaissance *emblemata* showing a terrible impossible group of intertwined images that don't make sense and yet are the motto, the coat of arms, the basic family raised to the dignity of an emblem which sustains. . . . Problems sustain us—maybe that's why they don't go away. What would a life be without them? Completely tranquillized and loveless, too. There is a secret love hiding in each problem. . . . We saw this happening in this interview. We started off with a little problem—could we do it, how to do it, did we, did I, want to do it—and as we went on, the problem kept us here, talking, working, meeting each other. And it became a product, a child. We made an interview. But in fact the interview preceded us, and it began as a problem. We only came together because of the interview, the imagination of an interview, the fantasy of it as an emblem that drew us together across the ocean, across the Alps, and we are both now attached and joined by it, a third, and we will be very loyal and try very hard to help it from now on with editors and publishers and readers, and it will last longer than we will, sustaining us, this third, loving us in return.

L.P.   *If we consider this last part of the interview as an ending, then we must say that, as in many Renaissance dialogues, we are ending on love. After the subject was gone into in detail, then love came with images of upward movement, hymns to love and beauty in the Platonic style. Without realizing it, we went back to it. . . .*

J.H.   Oh, yes, we went back to it but again with a slight twist, which is remembering the pathology of it. Not being worried about the pathologizing of it and of putting love down because it has this pathology, recognizing that within that love, it isn't only the wings, but they are also burnt. And there's also a twistedness and a hurt that goes with all loving. People know very well about this; they say, "It's all right as long as we don't hurt anyone"— but it will hurt, it has to hurt. So we are not ending with a paean or simply the praise of love as an ascension but the enjoyment of the pathologizing of love, too. And that's what keeps us psychoanalytic, modern: the sense that pathologies are forms of loving, ways of entering love, and that it, the pathology, loves us. That's why it clings to us. Hard to believe, but the hypochondrias are taking care of us, the depressions are slowing us down, obsessions are ways of polishing the image, paranoid suspicions are ways of trying to see through—all these moves of the pathological are ways we are being loved in the peculiar way the psyche works.

L.P.   *We can't seem to leave the old tale of Eros and Psyche which you have held to be the myth of analysis: psyche is always attracting love while eros is always trying to find soul, so that everything the soul does, no matter how pathological, is lovable, and everything erotic, no matter how pathological, is psychological.*

J.H.   Love isn't personal—that's the main point and that's what we keep forgetting. That's its main delusion, its main hysteria. Because it isn't yours, it isn't mine. It probably doesn't even belong to the Gods. Eros was not himself a God. The notion of love is strange, very foreign to the character of a God in the Greek context, in the context of most cultures, except Christianism. That's supposed to be Christianity's virtue, its uniqueness: Christianity made love into its God. So, to stay in touch with our culture's God, we have to feel love, be in love, be lovable, love others and ourselves as a commandment, and then love becomes a huge problem, the main effort of therapy. The love problem in a Christian culture is all wrapped up with saving our souls and finding God. Even this conversation now, that we are talking so much about love, has us right in this trap of our Christian culture. If we could only let love alone. If we could only give it more space and less attention, it would take care of itself. It's like having a friend in the house: don't badger him making him comfortable. Or a patient: don't keep taking his temperature. If we could just get out of the way, let it come, let it go. We are always trying to direct love into channels, "relating" it, "sharing" it ... ugh. Why?

L.P.   *Why? We are afraid of it.*

J.H.   ... it's ready to break out any minute. And what it wants is psyche. It's after soul, it has a job to do on the soul. I mean, love is far more interested in our fantasies, in our images and complexes, than it is in us, personally, what we feel and need and long for. So we are deathly afraid. It starts all the complexes jumping. It makes our fantasies irresistible, gilds them. Golden Aphrodite, they called her. Glowing. Burning. But love isn't some independent force outside the images, outside the complexes. It's right inside them, the eros is already right there inside the psyche, ready to break into fire. The psyche is a highly flammable material. So we are always wrapping things in asbestos, keeping our images and fantasies at arm's length because they are so full of love. See: Freud was right—the content of the repressed psyche is eros. And resistance has to do with fire-resistant walls. Naturally, everyone backs off from analysis, from their dreams and their figures like Mary Bell. They are packed with love. But the way into loving isn't direct, you can't go straight at it. And therapies that encourage love, that focus on transference make that mistake of going straight at it. At least for me the way is via the soul, the images, where love is hiding anyway.... Just start talking with anyone from the soul, about the soul, about your fear of dying, about a heartbreaking memory, about your funny estrangements, isolation, and right away love starts happening. Naturally, it breaks out in therapy sessions: wherever there is psyche there is amor, eros, love. Love comes into therapy to find psyche, to become psychological, and it really is a psychological mistake to take love personally. Of course, it feels personal, because love is interior, intimate, but this innerness refers to the soul, the activation of the complexes.

The alchemists said that as you go on with the work, soul work, soul-making, "its love will increase in you." They didn't say you will love more or better, they didn't say the work will love you more, that you will find love, be loved. I think they were referring to the strange fact that as you become occupied with the psyche, there is this "increase." The soul grows with a vegetable love, a mineral love—and, of course, an animal love which we are closer to and recognize more. But this increase is not an increase of consciousness. It's not an increase like maturation and development: the "growth" fantasy. Underneath these humanistic, these secular ideas, there is an alchemical activity going on in the plant kingdom, in the mineral kingdom, as if the leaves on the trees just come out in the spring because they love to, as if rubies and emeralds grow in the rocks like drops of intense love, as if the rocks themselves are full of desire, reaching toward some crystalline intensity, some luminosity inside themselves. Now all this takes heat, terrible pressure inside the tree branch, inside the ore, so we fall in love and blush red and get hot pants—that's the alchemical love increasing in you. Very concrete. Very physical, because it's inside nature itself.

The Buddha's supposed to have said there's fear in all things— well, isn't that the eros working inside the thing, intensifying it into an intelligible image, into psychic stuff, and the thing resists? It's afraid. The ore wants to stay just as it is; that is the nature of substance as Spinoza defined it—the desire to persist just as you are. I don't believe there can be love without fear. But these emotions aren't you—or it's a very different kind of you, not that *Io* and that *Sé,* that ego and self, but you as a kind of object of what's going on, or vessel in which the increase is building. You are being made by the desire in your own bedrock which is, of course, nothing else than your complexes, your problems, your unalterable bedrock pathologies. That's where the heat is and that's also where the increase of love is going on.

L.P.   *As we go through the pathologies of love, seeming to get worse, there is an "increasing," a "getting better." It's like the old saying: for anything to get better, it must first get worse. If we are afraid of getting worse, in this sense, that increase of love can't happen. This means that pathologies are necessary for loving.*

J.H.   No question—and that's partly why we have spent so much time talking about pathologies. But now we can see that we have had to pay them all this attention because they are the bedrock of loving.

L.P.   *I keep feeling that the pathologies get better as the love increases and that we are now talking about healing.*

J.H.   Maybe we shouldn't use those words "better" and "worse." Maybe only the word "increase," trying to understand the increase of love in an alchemical sense, trying to clarify this increase as if the rubies and the emeralds were clarifications of the ores, moments of intelligence that crystallize like insights in the middle of some dumb, dense love problem when the heat is really on. What I am trying to get at here is something beyond increase of love as compassion or the sympathy of all things as it was called once, beyond even that goal of therapy I have often mentioned: Alfred Adler's *Gemeinschaftsgefühl,* communal feeling, because it is beyond feeling and beyond even the extension of feeling into infinity and that quality of boundlessness—which can be after all just a wider subjectivism. I think the increase is more an intensity, but I don't mean passion, either, but more the recognition of the importance of any single moment, a moment become an image, any moment when something clarifies and there is such beauty and peace and joy and excitement.

You can call this healing, you can call it transformation—there are all sorts of names. But let's stay with the word "love" because

it is so amazing to realize that love is working toward clarification, that's its intention, and all the ferment, all the seething, is
its "increase," becoming clarified like a broth, like a butter, because what happens is transparency. And when we try to "clear
things up," go over the past to see it better, or put ourselves
through confessions—all that is part of love becoming clarified.
We are working at transparency. Impossible dark spots of the
interior person get lit up, the shadow, the ugliest man, all the
shames and embarrassments regarding the concealed personal
tied-up self—well, there they are. "Good morning! How are you!
Nice to see you!" They aren't gone away or healed or integrated.
Those hysterias you mentioned, those delusions. There they are,
but they have become transparent, for a moment at least, like
rubies and emeralds. The leopard can't change his spots, but the
spots can be gems. I am trying to say that your shadow is your
virtue, and that is what love is mostly about. And that's what
remains—if anything has to remain—after a person's dead. His
faults, his unbearable qualities, or hers, become clarified, and you
remember them as virtues. They stand out sharp and clear, like
essences. It's amazing how the very thing you couldn't bear in
your mother or father, in your wife or husband—they die, and
then the rubies show right in the shadow. . . .

And we have been trying to get at this in the interview: to let
the shadow into it, all the egocentric confessions and inflated
ideas, all the anima and animus, your kinds of questions and my
kinds of opinions, our terrible limitations as people, the limitations that belong to our natures, our leopard spots. . . . Oh, I don't
think we've clarified ourselves, but I do feel that something alchemical has been going on and that the soul has had a hand in it
all along, so that the embarrassment and shame and being afraid,
the revealing and confessing, was all part of building the intensity toward clarification, which means that maybe what we were
doing was part of love increasing.

L.P. *Our talk seems to insist on going back to the model or form
of the classical dialogue that we spoke about at the beginning, a
dialogue that not only ends with love, but seems to be doing so
self-consciously. We cannot escape tradition.*

J.H. Very Platonic, too. We have even introduced a myth of love. . . .

L.P. *You mean the myth of the rubies and the emeralds?*

J.H. I was thinking of transparency, of clarification. I was thinking that we aren't ending with Platonic wings or with Christian redemption, but with something very earthly. It's not puer, either, even though there is all this talk of fire, these fiery ideas. It's earthly because we have been struggling with some pretty hard ores, very concrete. Syndromes and therapy; and how to work and write; Italy. Those huge heavy figures of Freud and Jung—to say nothing of the Jungians! Even my own biography. These are very hard, very tough materials, that we've tried to clarify. That's what your questions were doing, and that's what my ramblings were trying to get at: clarify my complexes about the puer, about Dallas, about Christianity. And we were pushed into concrete life. We kept speaking of that concrete life in terms of therapy, but therapy is really a disguise for life itself. So the drive to explain each of these things was to make them more transparent. And we're pretty well done now; time's up. Which is right because the more things get clarified, the less you need to see through, figure things out, their psychological motives and histories and psychodynamics. Just images. Nothing more to say. Transparency is the end of psychology. It's all right there, like those miraculous underwater creatures whose bodies are all translucent jelly, dissolved in their own transparency so you can see right into their interiors, and their inner organs are vivid bright colors. Nothing to hide because what is there is so lovely.

L.P. *Like rubies and emeralds.*

J.H. At the same time they're just livers and stomachs.

L.P. *What about the ruses and concealment you said earlier were necessary for honest revelation?*

J.H. That jellyfish is a pretty slippery creature. How do we tell what is revelation and what is camouflage?

L.P. *Camouflage is revelation too because each person has his or her own way of hiding. Camouflage is simply another way of revealing yourself.*

J.H.   So there's no hiding possible in an interview. Good. That keeps it transparent.

L.P.   *Maybe it will feel to you, to us both, too transparent because anyone can hear the tapes or read the book and see the inner organs—the complexes and pathologies. In therapy what becomes transparent at least stays private to the consulting room, but an interview has the public in mind.*

J.H.   So it's out in public like my dream of doing analysis on the street corner. Entertainment—and no angel rushing by, no Platonic vision of higher things. Still, something important did happen even if *we* as people are still right here with plenty of shadow showing—livers and stomachs and leopard spots—the interview itself may have found *its* redemption. It wants to return to love, as you said; and that's why we kept trying to place the interview against a classical, a Renaissance background. But it's not these historical models, not even the Platonic model—what's really at the base of it all is love. And all the hiding and seeking, the pushing and pulling between us, were for *its* sake, intensifying it, increasing it to make *its* form more clear.

L.P.   *If the archetypal background of the interview is love, if its genre—which we wanted to discover at the beginning—takes its form from love, or has love at its origin, then it will be very hard to conclude an interview. It seems to want to go on; it seems to have a life of its own . . .*

J.H.   . . . because it wants to keep on generating, leading us into discovering things. All along it was generating our behavior and leading us, for instance, to talk in an interview style, an interview rhetoric. I thought at the beginning it was up to me, up to us, but we didn't make the interview; it made us. We are simply doing what *it* wants, appearing in it just as it wants us to be. It made us able to sit here together and get the job done and enjoy it, enjoy each other. There's the love right there. It's as if the genre, the interview as a living thing, has got us caught in it. So, we simply have to stop talking because the interview can hardly go on without us, *and* we have to ask the interview, say to it, "Thank you, Interview, but that's it—we have to go now. Please let us stop right here."

INDEX

Jung *(cont.)*
  differences between Hillman and,
    30–33
  first reading of, 95, 96
  Hillman's recollections of, 102–5
Jungian psychology (Jungian school),
    27–36, 39, 40, 57, 95, 104, 136, 146,
    147
  Christianity and, 82–84
  the self in, 82–83
Jung Institute, 99, 106–7

Kohut, H., 37, 38

Lacan, Jacques, 78, 84, 85
Laing, R. D., 156–57
Language
  conceptual, 55–57
  of feelings, 43–45
  mythical, 42
  psychological, 40–44, 155–56
Leisure, 172–73
Love, 177–94
  analysis and, 178–83, 189–92
  Christianity and, 189
  community and, 183–84
  falling or being in, 177–78
  friendship, 184–86
  generativity and, 186–87
  for images, 181–83
  increase of, 190–92
  interview and, 186, 192–94
  kinds of, 182–83
  loyalty as style of, 184
  narcissism and, 181–82
  problems (pathologies) and, 187,
    191, 192
  the third and, 186–88
  transference, 178–79
Loyalty, 184

Madness, 23–24. *See also* Psychosis
Mann, Thomas, 6
Masochism, 15
Masturbation, 12
Meditation, cults of, 141–42
Mediterranean fantasy, 2
Michelangelo, 19
Midrash, 28, 80
Miller, David, 77
Money, work and, 171
Monotheism, 78–79. *See also*
  Christianity
Moodiness, 19
Mythical language, 42
Myth of Analysis, The (Hillman), 65,
  158, 159
Myths (mythological behavior), 24
  Christianity and, 84
  Greek, 84
  the soul and, 26

Narcissism, love and, 181–82
Neurosis, 25
Nihilism, 140–42
Nominalism, 40–41
Now-culture (the Now), 114–17

Objects (things), 131–37
Obsessions, 22
Old and New (senex and puer),
  114–23
Opposites, 13–15
Opus, Jung's idea of, 168–69

Pain, awareness and, 15
Pathologizing, 20, 23, 26
Pathology, gods and, 25
Perfection, work and fiction of, 173–75
Person, concept of, 150–51
Personal relationships, 125. *See also*
  Friendship; Love
Perspective, notion of, 116–17
Petrarch, 19, 20
Platonic dialogue, 5, 8
Pleasure, 16
Plutarch, 8
Problems, love and, 187, 191, 192
Psychoanalysis, *see* Analysis; Therapy
Psychodynamics, 37–38
Psychological, meaning of the term,
  48–49
Psychology
  language of, 40–44, 155–56
  sensuous (aesthetic) basis for,
    144–45
  see also Archetypal psychology;
    Jungian psychology
Psychopathy, in American culture,
  126–28
Psychosis, 24–25. *See also* Madness
Puer archetype, 59–60
  re-union of senex and, 120–21
  senex and (old and new), 114–23
  work and, 172–73
  writings on, 146–47

Questioning, as working, 162

Religion, *see* Christianity; Monotheism
Renaissance, the, 19, 119–20, 145
Repression, 45–47, 125
Respect, 118–19
Re-Visioning Psychology (Hillman),
  147–53, 158
Revolution, 143–45
Rhetoric, 119
  of Jung and Freud, 156–57
  sickness as, 41, 42

Santayana, George, 90
School of psychology, founding a,
  27–28, 33–34